FARRAR
STRAUS
GIROUX

A GLORIOUS DEFEAT

A
GLORIOUS
DEFEAT

MEXICO AND ITS WAR WITH
THE UNITED STATES

TIMOTHY J. HENDERSON

HILL AND WANG
A division of Farrar, Straus and Giroux
New York

Hill and Wang
A division of Farrar, Straus and Giroux
19 Union Square West, New York 10003

Printed in the United States of America
First edition, 2007

Library of Congress Cataloging-in-Publication Data
Henderson, Timothy J.
    A glorious defeat : Mexico and its war with the United States /
Timothy J. Henderson.— 1st ed.
        p.   cm.
    Includes bibliographical references and index.
    ISBN-13: 978-0-8090-6120-4 (hardcover : alk. paper)
    ISBN-10: 0-8090-6120-1 (hardcover : alk. paper)
    1. Mexican War, 1846–1848—Causes.   2. Mexican War, 1846–
1848—Diplomatic history.   3. Mexico—Politics and government—
1821–1861.   4. Mexico—Foreign relations—1821–1861.   5. Mexico—
Foreign relations—United States.   6. United States—Foreign
relations—Mexico.   7. Mexican War, 1846–1848—Influence.
8. Mexico—History, Military—19th century.   I. Title.

E407 .H46 2007
973.6'2—dc22

                                                            2006031337

Designed by Debbie Glasserman

www.fsgbooks.com

16 18 20 19 17 15

FOR KARREN

War as a means of making an honorable peace was and is a rigorous duty of the government and of the nation . . . However lamentable and deplorable the rigors of war may be, Mexico cannot and must not purchase peace at any price other than that of blood. Defeat and death on the banks of the Sabine would be glorious and beautiful; a peace treaty signed in Mexico's National Palace would be infamous and execrable . . . *War at all cost!* That is our cry: War to secure the peace, to wash away an old insult, to ensure our future security.

—*El Siglo Diez y Nueve*, November 30, 1845

CONTENTS

Illustrations can be found on pages 105–112.

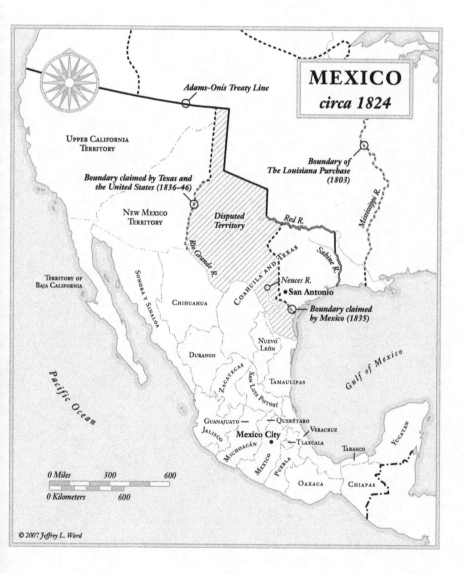

MEXICO
circa 1824

Adams-Onís Treaty Line

UPPER CALIFORNIA
TERRITORY

Boundary of
The Louisiana Purchase
(1803)

Boundary claimed by Texas and
the United States (1836–46)

NEW MEXICO
TERRITORY

Disputed
Territory

Red R.

Mississippi R.

TERRITORY OF
BAJA CALIFORNIA

SONORA Y SINALOA

CHIHUAHUA

Rio Grande R.

COAHUILA AND TEXAS

Sabine R.

Neuces R.

San Antonio

Boundary claimed
by Mexico (1835)

NUEVO
LEÓN

Pacific Ocean

DURANGO

ZACATECAS

SAN LUIS POTOSÍ

TAMAULIPAS

Gulf of Mexico

GUANAJUATO

QUERÉTARO

JALISCO

Mexico City

VERACRUZ

YUCATAN

MICHOACÁN

MEXICO

TLAXCALA

TABASCO

PUEBLA

OAXACA

CHIAPAS

0 Miles   300   600

0 Kilometers   600

© 2007 Jeffrey L. Ward

CHRONOLOGY

1819	Adams-Onís Treaty is signed; Moses Austin gets permission to start Texas colony.
1821	Mexico gains its independence.
1822	Stephen F. Austin seeks confirmation of his father's grant from authorities in Mexico City.
1823	Mexico's first colonization law is passed.
1824	Federalist constitution becomes law of Mexico.
1825	Joel Roberts Poinsett is appointed U.S. ambassador to Mexico.
1826	Fredonian Revolt in Texas.
1827–1828	Texas Boundary Commission investigates Texas, under leadership of General Manuel de Mier y Terán.
1828	Rebellion of La Acordada ousts Manuel Gómez Pedraza in favor of Vicente Guerrero.
1829	Mexico defeats Spanish expeditionary force; Guerrero is ousted; Joel Poinsett is expelled.
1830–1832	First Bustamante (centralist) government.
1830	Law of April 6, 1830, is passed.
1831	Vicente Guerrero rebels against Bustamante, is executed in February.

1831–1832   Tariff disturbances in Texas.

1832   Santa Anna rebels in name of federalism; General Terán commits suicide; Anastasio Bustamante is overthrown.

1833   Santa Anna is elected president; leaves power to Vice President Valentín Gómez Farías, who carries out liberal reforms; Stephen F. Austin travels to Mexico City to seek reforms.

1834   Santa Anna ousts Gómez Farías, institutes centralized regime.

1834–1835   Stephen Austin in prison.

1835–1836   Texas Revolution.

1836   Bustamante is elected president; revokes legislation implemented by Santa Anna and denounces Texas treaties.

1838   "Pastry War" with France; Santa Anna is rehabilitated.

1841   Rebellion overthrows Bustamante, makes Santa Anna provisional president.

1842   Santa Anna dissolves congress, rules as dictator; several skirmishes in Texas.

1843   Texas president Sam Houston declares unilateral armistice with Mexico.

1844   Santa Anna is overthrown in Three-Hour Revolution; José Joaquín de Herrera becomes president of Mexico; United States offers annexation to Texas.

1845   Mexico agrees to recognize Texas on condition it not be annexed to the United States; Texas rejects Mexico's offer, opts for annexation to the United States; Herrera is overthrown by Mariano Paredes y Arillaga; James K. Polk is elected president of the United States.

1845–1846   Mission of John Slidell to seek "boundary adjustment" with Mexico is not received by Mexican government.

1846   April 25—Skirmish in disputed territory leads President Polk to declare war.
             May 8—Battle of Palo Alto.
             May 9—Battle of Resaca de la Palma.
             July—Liberal revolt leads to return of Santa Anna from exile.
             September 20–24—Battle of Monterrey.

1847   February 20–23—Battle of Buena Vista.
             March 9–29—Battle of Veracruz.
             April—Gómez Farías is pushed out of office; General Pedro María Anaya is named interim president by Santa Anna.
             April 18—Battle of Cerro Gordo.
             August 20—Battles of Contreras and Churubusco.
             September 8—Battle of Molino del Rey.
             September 13—Battle of Chapultepec.
             September 14—Forces of General Winfield Scott take Mexico City.
             September—Santa Anna resigns as president and exiles self out of Mexico.
             November—General Pedro María Anaya is elected to presidency.

1848   January—Negotiations for peace begin.
             February 2—Treaty of Guadalupe Hidalgo is signed.
             March 10—Treaty of Guadalupe Hidalgo is ratified by U.S. Congress.
             May 30—Treaty of Guadalupe Hidalgo is ratified by Mexican congress.
             July 15—Last U.S. troops leave Mexico.

This book seeks to explain why Mexico went to war with the United States in 1846, and why that war went so badly for Mexico. Enthusiasts for military history should be fore-warned: even though the book ostensibly is about "war," it spends relatively little time detailing military maneuvering, focusing instead on political and diplomatic maneuvering. This is not to suggest that the mechanics of warfare were irrelevant; it is, rather, to suggest that an examination of how and why Mexico and the United States went to war sheds light on the conflict's real significance. It explains, for example, how both sides used specious arguments to justify the war, why the outcome was so lopsided, and why the war had such far-reaching consequences.

Most of what little literature is available on the U.S.-Mexican War in English deals primarily with military matters and tells the tale almost exclusively from the U.S. point of view. This book, by contrast, privileges the other side. While most readers are likely aware that the United States went to war with Mexico to gain territory and fulfill its "Manifest

Destiny," they will be far less certain why Mexico went to war with the United States.

One explanation holds that the Mexicans went to war because they were proud to the point of delusion, arrogantly overestimating their own strength. In fact, however, most of the Mexican politicians who led their country to war had a sober sense of their country's strengths and weaknesses, and few imagined that Mexico would prevail in a war with the United States. They led their country to war just the same, largely because of the gaping divisions in race, class, and ideology that prevented Mexico from being truly a "nation," and because they seethed in the daunting shadow of a powerful, wealthy, and aggressive neighbor.

I make no effort to resolve the question of which side—the United States or Mexico—was to "blame" for the war. There were cynical, shortsighted, unethical, reckless, and bigoted leaders on both sides, and there was plenty of blame to go around. Mexico's weakness with respect to the United States, which lay at the root of the conflict, was no one's fault but was rather the result of a long and complex history.

While according to nearly every economic and social indicator, Mexico was weaker than the United States, merely to assert this fact would be unenlightening. To paraphrase Tolstoy, every weak country is weak in its own way. Understanding the root causes of Mexico's weakness is crucial. Mexico began its independent life with a host of formidable obstacles to achieving coherent nationhood—obstacles that the United States simply did not have to face. At first glance Mexico seems to have begun its independent life as a proud and optimistic empire but descended within a decade into complete anarchy. As historian Timothy Anna points out, however, it is probably more accurate to see the process going on in those decades not as an unraveling but rather as a kind of groping toward nationhood—a series of halting attempts to overcome the obstacles created by the many disparate regions, races, cultures, and classes that made up Mexico and to forge a common identity. This book, then, rather than trying to assign blame, seeks to understand Mexico's weakness and how that weakness helped to land it in a war with the United States.

That such a book is needed has been brought home to me by some of the frenzied rhetoric that swirls around U.S.-Mexican relations in our own day. The disparity in wealth and power between the United States and Mexico—which, of course, remains very much intact—has given rise to many problems, including massive immigration from Mexico into the United States, much of it illegal. The immigration issue periodically flares into heated debate, as it did while I was completing this book. On the American far right some hysterically characterize Mexican immigration as an "invasion." One fringe group even conjures the specter of a "Conquest of Aztlán," charging that the Mexican government is actively abetting a conspiracy to retake the lands it lost to the United States in 1848. And while some imagine an insidious takeover of the U.S. Southwest, others look with equal virulence in the other direction. A letter to the editor of the Greensboro News & Record, written in the immediate aftermath of the U.S. invasion of Iraq, proposed, without a hint of drollery, that the United States follow up on the Iraq venture by invading Mexico. "Since we have no way to stop [Mexican immigration]," this citizen wrote, "why not invade Mexico and make it our 51st state?"[1]

What such views have in common is a profound indifference toward Mexico's realities and a thorough lack of respect for its people. If Mexicans desperate for work enter the United States, they are derided as a horde and a contagion. If Americans, on the other hand, should enter Mexico with hostile intent, it is assumed their cause must be righteous and that the Mexicans would be too pusillanimous to resist. It is quite possible that the U.S.-Mexican War had the pernicious effect of helping to instill in Americans the notion that the world's peoples are a perfectly pliant mass and that invading and incorporating foreign lands is an easy and painless undertaking. Subsequent U.S. experiences in the Philippines, Cuba, Vietnam, and Iraq have abundantly belied this notion, but the lesson, it seems, never quite gets learned. Historians second-guess the past at their peril, but it seems safe enough to suggest that had the United States chosen to remain in Mexico after the war, the results would have been catastrophic. Most of the Mexicans who fought in the war against the United States had little incentive to defend a government that did not represent them and that, in fact, despised them. That does not mean they would have welcomed U.S. domination.

The war between the United States and Mexico ended up being costly for both countries. Apart from the obvious costs in blood and treasure, the war accelerated social and political processes that eventually plunged both countries into bitter civil wars. It also left a legacy of mistrust and resentment between the United States and Mexico, as well as between the United States and the rest of its hemispheric neighbors. A recent minor diplomatic flare-up helps to illustrate the point. Marine Lance Corporal Juan López Rangel, the son of Mexican parents who had migrated to a small town in Georgia, was killed in the Iraq war on June 21, 2004. His parents decided to have his remains buried in his hometown, San Luis de la Paz, in the state of Guanajuato, Mexico. The ceremony, which took place over the July 4 weekend, was supposed to feature a Marine Corps Honor Guard carrying ceremonial weapons. But just short of the gravesite, a dozen Mexican soldiers stopped the honor guard and demanded that they surrender their "weapons." When the Marines refused, they were escorted to their cars and held under armed guard until the funeral ceremony was concluded. The presence of armed American soldiers on Mexican soil, it would seem, still arouses strong feelings, even when their weapons are fake and their intent is respectful.

The tempest that followed the incident is also telling. The U.S. ambassador to Mexico called Lance Corporal López a "hero" and expressed outrage over the scene at the gravesite.

That outrage was rejoined in letters to Mexico's left-leaning newspapers by those who saw Corporal López as at best a victim of U.S. aggression and at worst an agent of U.S. imperialism. "Our heroes," read one letter to a national newspaper, "are not the traitors who join the American army but those Mexicans who fought the Americans when they invaded our country in 1846."[2]

Ulysses S. Grant, who served as a young second lieutenant during the U.S.-Mexican War, late in his life famously described that war as "one of the most unjust ever waged by a stronger against a weaker nation."[3] The sentiment might well have been sincere, but at roughly the same time he wrote those words, Grant was in the forefront of plotting a commercial assault on Mexico. In an interview he assured potential U.S. investors that the Mexican people were "industrious, frugal, and willing to work for even a pittance, if afforded an opportunity."[4] That Grant considered the Mexicans' most remarkable characteristic to be their capacity to work hard for a pittance suggests that he exemplified a peculiar strain of American hubris. Throughout history, it seems, American interest in Mexico has been conditioned by Mexico's ability to benefit or menace the United States. A true collaboration based on mutual respect and an understanding of our common history would be a welcome change, one that would surely help to resolve vexing problems on both sides of the border. I hope this book, in some small way, will contribute to such a change.

A NOTE ON PLACE NAMES

I have chosen to refer to places by the names that are most familiar to American readers. Thus San Antonio de Béxar, commonly known as Béxar when Texas was a Mexican state, I call San Antonio. Likewise, the river that Mexicans call the Río Bravo del Norte is herein referred to as the Rio Grande.

A GLORIOUS DEFEAT

THE UNITED STATES AND MEXICO,

CIRCA 1821

Mexico gained its independence from Spain in 1821, at a time when the United States was the world's oldest and most successful federal republic. In those days Mexico and the United States were very roughly comparable in size and population, and among the leadership of both countries there were enthusiasts for the ideals of progress, reason, science, and democracy. It is true that the United States was easily twice as wealthy as Mexico, but Mexicans tended to attribute this disparity to Spain's tyrannical mismanagement of its colonial economy. With independence, they expected soon to close the gap.

In fact, however, any similarities between the two nations were superficial, while the differences were profound—and all of the differences worked to Mexico's disadvantage. Some knowledge of those differences is essential to understanding why Mexico and the United States went to war in 1846, and why that war went so disastrously for Mexico.

DIFFERING LEGACIES

The United States and Mexico had both been colonies of European powers, but they were heirs to very different colonial legacies. Britain had distanced itself far more thoroughly from the medieval heritage than had Spain: it had limited the power of its monarchy, nurtured a robust private sector, championed the impersonal rule of law, and broken the religious monopoly of the Roman Catholic Church. A good portion of the British elite embraced the ideas of the eighteenth-century Enlightenment, and Britain's colonists eagerly seconded that embrace. That is, many of the most prominent leaders in Britain and its colonies believed that reason should trump tradition; that progress and change should be welcomed rather than feared; that individuals should be equal before a clearly codified law and free to advance in life on the basis of merit rather than bloodlines; that sovereignty should be more or less popular and government should incorporate checks and balances as safeguards against corruption and tyranny; that wealth was not finite but was infinitely expandable through free trade, which would reward hard work and ingenuity, and that even the poor could prosper if they energetically pursued their own material self-interest; that the trend toward increasing social equality was something to be welcomed; and that citizens should be free to believe, say, and publish whatever they wished. Enthusiasm for such ideas—collectively known during the nineteenth century as "liberalism"—created a powerful bond among the ruling classes of the British Empire, one that would stand the founders of the North American republic in good stead as they forged their new nation.

While one group of Mexican leaders greatly admired all of the enlightened notions that so captivated the founders of the United States, another group of entrenched Mexican oligarchs clung to medieval habits with a ferocious tenacity.

Even if there had been a consensus that liberal ideals were desirable, conditions in Mexico made it far more difficult for the Mexicans to implement liberal policies. When the French nobleman Alexis de Tocqueville praised the United States Constitution—the first instance of liberalism codified as a national charter—he described it as "one of those beautiful creations of human diligence which give their inventors glory and riches but remain sterile in other hands." To illustrate what he meant by "other hands," he asked his readers to consider the case of Mexico, which adopted a similar charter in 1824 and experienced only "anarchy" and "military despotism."[1] To a far greater extent than Anglo-America, Hispanic America clung to a tradition where rights were defined by inherited privilege; where social inequalities were said to be established by God and were considered necessary to maintain social peace; where the king made all important decisions; where law was chaotic and readily abused; and where the economy functioned at the government's pleasure. In Mexico the colonial centuries had left a legacy perhaps too powerful to overcome, at least in the short term.

Differences in historical tradition were accentuated by sharp differences in land and people. Despite the self-serving claims of British American colonists that they had tamed a barren wilderness, the lands of North America were of course inhabited. But the natives were too scattered, weak, and unorganized to put up successful resistance, leaving them vulnerable to ruthlessly efficient extermination or relocation at the hands of whites. Nor was there a large, settled peasantry capable of stout resistance, such as existed in both Mexico and the Old World, so individual landownership and the pursuit of enlightened self-interest encountered fewer obstacles. British North America boasted its share of land barons, but big landowners were far from holding a monopoly of land, and unlike in Mexico there was no Roman Catholic Church claiming extensive corporate property and privilege. Accordingly, in the United States wealth circulated fairly freely, and ordinary citizens could hope to gain land and opportunity.

Few in British North America boasted titles of rank that set them much above their fellows. In contrast to the stuffy elitism of the Old World, lineage was of scant concern to the Anglo-Americans. People enjoyed differing levels of wealth and power, of course, but in general the poor in America were less poor than their Old World counterparts, and the rich were less rich. "No novelty in the United States struck me more vividly during my stay there," wrote Tocqueville in the 1830s, "than the equality of conditions. It was easy to see the immense influence of this basic fact on the whole course of society."[2]

Anglo-Americans tended also to believe that universal education not only inculcated the values of good citizenship but also aided economic growth and therefore should be universally available. In the early nineteenth century education was fast becoming available to all white, and even to a few black, Americans. By the 1830s the United States was among the world's most literate societies. Many Mexican leaders shared the sense that public education was vital to social health, but they encountered formidable obstacles to implementing successful educational programs, and the overwhelming majority of Mexicans remained illiterate throughout the nineteenth century.

Of course, in the United States slaves, Indians, and indentured servants were not held to be "equal" to free white Americans, and they did not enjoy citizenship rights. The enslavement of blacks and the dispossession of Indians were glaring exceptions to nearly every principle that U.S. elites claimed to hold dear, and these original sins would nearly capsize the republican experiment. That crisis, however, remained decades away. Indentured servants, at least, would gain freedom upon fulfilling their contracts, whereupon they merged into a free white population that afforded most of them considerable opportunity. Anglo-Americans scarcely entertained the idea that Indians and blacks should enjoy full citizenship rights and so believed that their interests could blithely be ignored. The politically engaged people of the United States were ethnically homogeneous. In the first decades after independence American leaders seldom tired of pointing out, with inordinate pride, that theirs was a republic of white men.

Mexico's social makeup was far more complicated and muddled than that of the United States, its past more violent and traumatic. Modern Mexico was born in 1521 amid the spectacular violence of the Conquest, where Spanish adventurers led by the intrepid conquistador Hernán Cortés laid waste to the opulent Aztec Empire, which claimed several million subjects. The capital of that empire, Tenochtitlán, was an engineering marvel, home to some two or three hundred thousand people, more than lived in contemporary Madrid or Paris. That great city was reduced to a stinking rubble after a months-long battle. The horror and devastation of the conquest was followed by a veritable holocaust for the native population: over the ensuing decades millions of Mexico's indigenous people perished from overwork and abuse and waves of epidemic Old World disease to which they had no immunity. Even so, the indigenous population was too large and stubborn to be eradicated or removed, so the Spaniards and Indians reached certain accommodations. Spaniards were heirs to a tradition wherein the conquered were made to serve the conquerors, which fit well with their plans and culture. Spanish gentlemen eschewed manual labor, but there was plenty of manual labor to be done—in the fields, in the mines, in the carrying trades. Simply put, nonwhites became the working classes of colonial Mexico, since white skin was all it took to elevate a man to the status of New World nobility.

For all their brutality and callousness, in fact the Spaniards were great innovators in the area of race relations. They were arguably the first people to seriously ponder the implications of intercultural contact on a vast scale. Yet while learned clerics at Spain's universities debated the worth of the Indian race, their counterparts, the bold missionaries to the New World, were busy carrying out an experiment in social engineering that, although done with compassionate intentions, had unfortunate consequences that are still felt today. They deemed the native peoples of America to be perpetual children, fledglings whose tender wings would never permit them to leave the nest. Accordingly, they designed a paternalistic regime full of special protections and a few onerous requirements, one that inculcated dependence and a fair degree of isolation from white society. Indians held certain inalienable communal lands, lived in semiautonomous villages, had law courts designed specifically to hear their charges and complaints, were not permitted to carry guns or swords, could not enter the priesthood or other professions, were not permitted to borrow more than five pesos, and were required to pay a race-based head tax. Relying on such blatant paternalism, the friars hoped to protect the Indians as far as possible from the corrupting influence of white civilization.

In some ways they succeeded all too well. Indians lived in self-governing villages; most did not learn Spanish or adopt many Spanish ways; they were able to preserve many of their pre-Columbian beliefs and practices, albeit in somewhat distorted forms; they remained, for the most part, desperately poor and outside the market economy; and their interactions with people from outside their culture were limited and characteristically hostile. All of this remained largely true as Mexico entered the nineteenth century and the era of its independent existence. Policymakers in Mexico thus confronted obstacles that their neighbors to the north did not. The Indians, who accounted for perhaps about 60 percent of the population, were unassimilated, illiterate, and unable to speak what white elites deemed to be the national language. One writer at the time of the U.S.-Mexican War reckoned that perhaps three-quarters of Mexico's indigenous population had not yet heard the news of Mexico's independence from Spain.

Some 22 percent of Mexico's population consisted of *castas*, a generic term for people of mixed race. The conquistador Hernán Cortés himself had helped kick off this trend by fathering an illegitimate son by his Indian interpreter, Doña Marina (better known to history as La Malinche). Other conquistadors and early settlers followed suit, bringing into being a class of *mestizos*, persons of mixed Indian and European blood. Adding to the racial mix were enslaved Africans, brought to work in the mines and on sugar plantations. Blacks, in turn, produced offspring with Indians and whites. (In Mexico such offspring were called *zambos* and *mulattos* respectively.) In a country that was in theory sharply divided by race—there was a "Republic of Spaniards" and a "Republic of Indians"—the castas fit into no officially recognized category. For the three hundred years of the Spanish colony, they inhabited the uncomfortable margins of society, with few opportunities for advancement. Only one institute of higher learning in all of Mexico admitted castas, the undistinguished Colegio de San Juan de Letrán, where the meager curriculum included courses in how to beg for alms.

Not surprisingly, castas tended toward fairly menial occupations: they became artisans, muleteers, hacienda overseers, domestic servants, and market vendors. The more they tried to gain respect and social standing, the more the whites insisted on their own racial "purity." In the late colonial era whites took to devising rather bizarre new racial designations based on the intricate intermingling of white, Indian, and African blood. The closer those mixtures came to whiteness, the more respectable they became, but it was never quite possible to erase the stain of nonwhite blood in the eyes of the white elite. By the time of Mexico's independence, castas were the fastest-growing element of the Mexican population, yet their status remained oddly undetermined. Their pretensions to power and respect would provoke some of the most gruesome episodes in the history of the early Mexican Republic.

Mexico's racial situation, then, was a good deal more complex than that of the United States. There was one blessing: by the end of the colonial era Mexico had relatively few enslaved blacks (some eight thousand, perhaps), most of them concentrated in the torrid coastal regions. The institution of slavery was entirely negligible to Mexico's economy. Mexico therefore was able to suppress that institution with relative ease, affording it one of its few advantages over its northern neighbor.

This single blessing, however, did not make Mexico's racial sins any less damning than those of the United States. The Indians and the castas suffered grotesque marginalization and poverty. Nineteenth-century visitors to Mexico City, who arrived expecting to experience the fabled elegance of the old colonial capital, were inevitably scandalized by the sight of thousands of dark-skinned people living out of doors and in the most appalling squalor: clad in dirty rags, covered with frightful sores and wounds, living from crime or begging. The well-to-do residents of the capital developed a colorful lexicon of disparaging terms to describe these despised people: *los léperos, la canalla, los sansculottes, la chusma, el populacho*—all translating, with varying shades of emphasis, to "the rabble." Brantz Mayer, who served as secretary of the U.S. legation in Mexico during the 1840s, left a vivid portrait of the famed Mexican *lépero*, with his long, vermin-infested hair, torn and stinking clothing, wild eyes, and "features pinched by famine into sharpness." Such people spent their days around the markets and shops that sold pulque—the fermented juice of the century plant that was the intoxicant of choice among Mexico's poor—"feeding on fragments, quarreling, drinking, stealing and lying drunk about the pavements, with their children crying with hunger around them."[3]

The relatively better-off working people of the city—who were mostly mestizo and were generally included in the category of "rabble"—tended to live in first-floor apartments that routinely flooded during the rainy season, contributing to a shockingly high mortality rate. Children under the age of three accounted for a third of all deaths in the city. In the countryside famine was a recurring nightmare, as were periodic epidemics of smallpox and *matlazahuatl*, a disease resembling smallpox that affected Mexico's Indian population exclusively. Some estimates place Mexico's illiteracy rate as high as 99 percent. Where Alexis de Tocqueville was impressed with the overwhelming equality he found in the United States, another European traveler, the German scientist Alexander von Humboldt, found the opposite in Mexico. He described it with brutal simplicity: "Mexico is the country of inequality. Nowhere does there exist such a fearful difference in the distribution of fortune, civilization, cultivation of the soil and population."[4]

Nature itself dealt rather perversely with Mexico, exacerbating that "fearful difference" of which Humboldt spoke and making it difficult for Mexicans to forge a cohesive nation. Most of Mexico's fertile land is concentrated in the tropical highlands at the country's center, and that area was home to the largest portion of the Mexican population. The remaining population was scattered throughout a rugged and often harsh landscape. The difficulties of transportation and the tremendous variation in land and resources helped to make Mexico a country of regions. Common allegiance to a remote king and an official Church afforded some coherence during the colonial period, but those bonds were weakened or destroyed with independence, and nothing appeared to replace them. Outside the capital city most Mexicans tended to identify with their own locality, often referred to as *la patria chica* or "little homeland." Family, community, and local political bosses mattered, while the nation as a whole remained a troublesome abstraction. While in the United States the land's topography contributed to social equality and national sentiment, in Mexico it encouraged diversity, inequality, and conflict. The midnineteenth-century writer Mariano Otero lamented this phenomenon in a sentence that seemed to encapsulate the woes that haunted his generation: "In Mexico there is not, nor is there a possibility of developing, a national spirit, because there is no nation." This exaggerated regionalism, joined to the appalling divisions of race and class, would emerge as one of the country's most intractable problems during its early decades, and it would contribute greatly to the outbreak and course of the U.S.-Mexican War.

Clearly, then, the United States and Mexico differed profoundly in their histories and social realities. Important differences prevailed in political traditions as well. The British North American colonies were self-governing to a far greater extent than were the Spanish American colonies. In British North America colonial assemblies functioned practically without interference from the mother country. Only landowners had the right to vote, but landownership was so pervasive that some 50 to 80 percent of all male colonists did indeed vote, and only about five percent of legislation coming out of the colonial assemblies was overturned in England. True, the American colonists had no representation in the British Parliament, and governors were generally royal appointees. Still, politics in the American colonies were assertive and robust, and there was broad agreement on the essential principle that sovereignty resided—or at least should rightly reside—with the people.

Mexico, meanwhile, was heir to one of western Europe's most intransigent monarchical traditions. From 1521, when King Charles I crushed a popular uprising at the Battle of Vil-

lalar, Spain—Mexico's imperial master—was resolutely devoted to the practice of royal absolutism. While creoles, as
American-born whites were called, might gain some limited
political experience on town councils, or perhaps even as
judges on the local governing bodies known as *audiencias*, the
political system was in essence a chaotic jumble of jurisdic-
tions maneuvering under the auspices of a powerful king and
his viceroy (the highest royal representative in the colonies).
One gained influence not through formal institutions such as
representative assemblies but through the informal channels
of blatant cronyism or trading on inherited privilege. Spain
was remarkably successful in excluding the colonists almost
entirely from imperial politics, leaving the leaders of independent Mexico with scant political experience and few viable
political traditions to draw from as they forged their new
state.

In both the United States and Mexico, religion could be
counted on to furnish a host of contentious issues, but those
issues were generally much less contentious in the former.
Many of the founders of the United States were deists, men
who believed that God took little or no active interest in his
creation and that humans must attend to their own destinies.
"It will forever be acknowledged," wrote John Adams in
1786, with perhaps a bit more optimism than was warranted,
"that these governments were contrived by reason and the
senses."[5] While religious intolerance might rear its ugly head
in various locales at different times, the United States generally came to enjoy a tradition of religious pluralism and toleration. If most of the Founding Fathers of the United States
were not notably religious, neither were they aggressively an-
tireligious, as they had no need to be. There was no official
church seeking to impede the aims of statesmen, no church
claiming enormous landholdings and entrenched wealth, no
clergy demanding political power and special privileges. The

United States was thus spared the immensely damaging phenomena of religious intolerance and "anticlericalism," as liberal hostility toward the Catholic Church and its clergy was known.

Anticlericalism was indeed a crippling feature of life in Mexico. Some—generally those who called themselves "liberals"—came to blame the Roman Catholic Church for many, if not most, of Mexico's problems. According to the standard liberal critique, the church monopolized large portions of the nation's resources, using them inefficiently and unproductively. The taxes the church collected, mostly in order to sustain a parasitic upper clergy and to maintain its opulent cult, diminished the liquid wealth of the nation. The church, liberals charged, was one of the principal bulwarks against true equality of all citizens, for it had been largely responsible for institutionalizing the system of castes, and priests tended to instruct the poor to accept their lot on earth gracefully in anticipation of a celestial reward. Priests, moreover, claimed the traditional *fuero*, which entitled them to immunity from prosecution under civil law—in the liberal view, a glaring impediment to the cherished goal of social equality. The clergy's allegiance to Rome, liberals believed, was an obstacle to national sovereignty, and Rome's claim that it had the right to appoint top clergymen threatened to subvert civil government at every turn. Moreover, liberals asserted, the church maintained unsanitary practices, such as interring the remains of pious elites in the walls and beneath the floors of cathedrals, and it was unalterably opposed to science, progress, and liberal political ideas, making free use of censorship and spiritual intimidation to uphold its dogmas.

Whether or not such charges were entirely true and fair—and there is ample evidence that they were exaggerated and oversimplified—critics of the church grew increasingly shrill as the nineteenth century progressed, and the clergy grew increasingly intransigent in the face of that criticism. The middle ground between the two sides gradually evaporated, leaving an almost unbridgeable chasm.

Still, if some Mexicans saw the church as an obstacle to progress, even many who criticized the church were in no hurry to accept religious toleration. Whereas in the United States a spirit of genuine nationalism—that is, a sincere devotion to the country and its ideals—grew steadily during the early decades of the nineteenth century, in Mexico relatively few had much sense of nationhood or allegiance to the country's central government. Under such circumstances religion seemed the only available substitute for patriotism. According to the leading conservative of the epoch, Lucas Alamán, religion provided the "only common link which binds all Mexicans, when all the rest have been broken."[6] Without the unifying and civilizing influence of the church, many assumed, Mexico's masses would give themselves over entirely to barbarism, and society would be plunged headlong into the direst anarchy. Before 1860 all Mexican law deemed Roman Catholicism to be the official religion, without tolerance of any other. Religious intolerance, in turn, stifled creativity and initiative, discouraged immigration, and contributed to Mexico's backwardness.

Finally, the United States and Mexico were heirs to very different economic legacies. The Anglo-Americans were profoundly influenced by British writers who were at the forefront of a move toward economic liberalism. They came to believe that economies functioned according to natural laws and that governmental interference in economic matters only impeded the functioning of those laws. If individuals were free to pursue their own interests, and if goods were allowed to circulate freely, the marketplace would regulate itself to the benefit of all. And while the unregulated market certainly had its pitfalls, this free trade ideology undeniably helped to undergird Britain's industrial revolution, which in turn brought a tremendous economic boom in the last half century of the

British American Empire. The United States, upon freeing itself from that empire, continued to enjoy vigorous international trade for decades into its independent life.

By contrast, the economy of the Spanish Empire was founded resolutely upon the principles of mercantilism. That is, Spanish imperialists held that the amount of the world's wealth was finite and that governments should interfere in all aspects of the economy so as to ensure for themselves as much of that wealth as possible. Other European colonial powers held to these same principles, but the Spaniards outdid them all in their overbearing insistence on economic control. Since mercantilists tended to measure wealth in terms of precious metals, the Spaniards focused almost monomaniacally on the exploitation of the rich silver mines of Peru and Mexico. Miners and merchants were organized into guilds that were licensed by the Spanish crown. Silver could be shipped only on authorized fleets leaving from authorized ports under heavy guard. Spain awarded itself an absolute monopoly on trade, which meant the colonies were forced either to pay exorbitant prices for consumer goods or to collaborate with smugglers abetted by Spain's enemies. The colonies were not permitted to trade among themselves; nor were colonists permitted to produce commodities that would compete with the ones produced in the mother country. One British economist of the late seventeenth century took Spain to task for such heavy-handed dealings with its colonies. "Future times," he wrote, "will find no part of the Story of this Age so strange, as that all the other States of *Europe* . . . have not combined together to enforce a liberty of Trade in the *West Indies*; the restraint whereof is against all Justice."[7]

During the eighteenth century the Bourbon kings of Spain experimented with some easing of these restrictions, but at the same time they dramatically increased taxes and systematically favored Spanish-born citizens over creoles for political appointments. Even at its most liberal the Spanish system seemed designed to inhibit entrepreneurship. The colonies were awash with irritating restrictions and regulations; the legal system was chaotic and arbitrary, ensuring that property rights were always ambiguous; privileged groups enjoyed special favors, and the nonprivileged suffered in the bargain; and vast amounts of land were tied up in entails belonging to the church or to Indian villages. According to one estimate, Spain's intrusions into its colonial economy cost its colonists thirty-five times more than Britain cost its North American colonies.[8] In sum, for three centuries Spain maintained the economies of its American colonies in a state of dependence and underdevelopment.

Mexico's poor economic performance after independence, however, cannot be blamed entirely on Spanish policies. Nature also contributed to Mexico's economic woes. The densely populated central plateau regions, home to most of the population, are interrupted by forbidding volcanic ridges and deep gullies, making transportation difficult and costly. To the east and west of the central plateaus, the land descends precipitously toward the sweltering lands of the coasts. To the north and south the drop-off is more gradual, but soon enough the lush highland landscape gives way to hot, hilly scrubland and dry desert. Mexico's principal port, Veracruz, is separated from the center by some 260 miles of notoriously rugged terrain. Road-building on such terrain would have been difficult even for a country of abundant wealth; for Mexico, it was a practical impossibility. Mexico also lacks navigable rivers, so the difficulty and high cost of transportation was a permanent brake on Mexico's economic progress. Fanny Calderón de la Barca, the wife of the Spanish ambassador to Mexico in the 1840s, was dismayed when she visited a farm on land that was both beautiful and fertile and found that farm to be "the picture of loneliness and desolation." The farm's owner explained that the local population was sparse and essentially self-sufficient, so the only possible market for his grain was Mexico City, more than a hundred miles away. Any profit he might have made would have been eaten up by transportation costs and taxes. And so both agriculture and industry languished.

The differences, then, between the United States and Mexico around 1821 could not be measured in a handful of statistics. During the nineteenth century the notions of reason, science, progress, equality, and freedom became identified with the very concept of modernity. The country with fewer obstacles to putting those notions into practice would have a major advantage in the race for preeminence. The United States entered its independent life with far less historical baggage than Mexico, and its experiments with new political, social, and economic forms were much more likely to succeed. Its population was more ethnically homogeneous and culturally unified than Mexico's; and while Americans considered their natural landscape an enticing vista with room to expand and develop new resources and markets, Mexicans found their landscape presented only maddening obstacles and generated endless conflict. In the first half of the nineteenth century the United States clearly would win the race for preeminence. In 1800 total income in the United States was merely twice that of Mexico, but by 1845 it was thirteen times greater. In short, as the United States grew more powerful and prosperous, Mexico descended into frustrating cycles of conflict, despotism, penury, and despair.

THE ROAD TO INDEPENDENCE

A final and extremely crucial difference between the United States and Mexico involved the two countries' routes to independence. Independence in the United States came about as the result of a bloody but purposeful war. The political and military leaders of the American independence movement became the nation's Founding Fathers, and they were able to

design the new republic in accordance with the Enlightenment values they largely shared. Mexico's experience was
more ambiguous and troubled.

Mexico's independence movement began much later than
that of the United States. This was not because Mexico's creoles (American-born whites) were pleased with their imperial
masters: the Spaniards had discriminated against the creoles,
restricted their economic activities, and taxed them mercilessly. Rather, the delay was caused principally by their fear of
the yawning gulf between the races and classes. Creoles were
white, and many lived in considerable comfort. They well understood that the dark-skinned, impoverished masses tended
to see little distinction between creoles and Spaniards: as far
as those masses were concerned, the two groups looked pretty
much alike, and both looked like the people responsible for
centuries of oppression and exploitation. A breakdown of order, the creoles understood, might well land them at the
mercy of angry mobs bent on vengeance.

In 1808 Napoleon Bonaparte's armies overran Spain, forcing the abdication of the Spanish king and his heir. Spaniards
immediately rose in arms against the usurpation, forming a
decidedly liberal movement that, in 1812, promulgated a
liberal constitution. The Spanish American colonists were
forced to choose between recognizing Napoleon's brother,
Joseph, as their king; striking out for independence; or taking
the more cautious course of forming caretaker governments
until the rightful king, Ferdinand VII, could be restored to
the Spanish throne. In Mexico the more cautious option was
chosen, and Mexico's government fell into the hands of very
conservative Spaniards.

On September 16, 1810, a fifty-seven-year-old priest
named Miguel Hidalgo launched a rebellion against that government. Unlike many of his fellow creoles, Hidalgo did not
doubt the wisdom of mobilizing the impoverished Indians
and castas to man his army. He summoned them to the main

square of the small town of Dolores and explicitly exhorted them to exact vengeance against the *gachupines* (an insulting term for Spaniards) for three centuries of humiliation and despoilment.

Unfortunately for the independence movement, the first engagements of Mexico's war of independence appeared to confirm more conservative creoles' worst fears. In the wealthy mining town of Guanajuato, Hidalgo's troops went on a rampage. Several hundred Spaniards were killed in the initial siege, and afterward the rebels indulged themselves in an orgy of looting, pillaging, murder, and mutilation. The scene was repeated about a month later at Guadalajara, though here the rebels increased the horror by decapitating their Spanish prisoners. To the comfortable classes of Mexico, it seemed as if the very sinews of civilization had been sundered. They compared these events to other well-known nightmares of modern times: the sans-culottes of the French revolution flooding the streets of Paris with the blood of aristocrats; the black slaves of Haiti rising up against their masters, the wealthy planters, carrying out brutal massacres and torching plantations. The leading conservative of early nineteenth-century Mexico, Lucas Alamán, who was an eyewitness to the siege of Guanajuato, would write decades later that the rebels' battle cry—"Long live the Virgin of Guadalupe and death to the *gachupines!*"—"after so many years . . . still resounds in my ears with a frightful echo!"

For conservative Mexicans, the lessons of the early course of the independence war were pivotal. First, these events resoundingly confirmed their suspicion that the vast majority of their fellow countrymen were irresponsible and dangerous and that therefore social control must be maintained at all costs; second, in Mexico the ideas that inspired these events—democracy, republicanism, equality, civil liberties—were impractical at best, lethal at worst. These conservatives, having stared into the gaping maw of barbarism, concluded that they themselves should hold a monopoly on political power. By the 1830s they had adopted a name for themselves: they were the *hombres de bien*—the men of goodness.

Hidalgo was captured and executed in 1811. His successor, a mestizo priest named José María Morelos, was captured and executed in 1815. Other leaders would follow, but the movement became negligible with Morelos's death. When independence did finally come to Mexico, it was largely a reaction *against* the liberal ideas championed by Hidalgo and Morelos.

It was, in fact, an archconservative royalist army officer who consummated independence after he had been fighting ruthlessly against it for a decade. Alarmed by a liberalizing movement in Spain, Brigadier General Agustín de Iturbide issued an invitation to the leader of the surviving rebel forces, General Vicente Guerrero, to join him in declaring Mexico's separation from Spain. On February 24, 1821, Iturbide promulgated his Plan of Iguala, a declaration of independence designed to please a very broad and varied constituency, from reactionary royalists and pious Catholics to liberal firebrands. The plan addressed only those issues on which there was already widespread agreement, or at least issues on which compromise was probable. The first three articles declared that Roman Catholicism was to be Mexico's official and only legal religion; that Mexico was an independent country; and that its government was to be a constitutional monarchy. Those three principles—religion, independence, and monarchy— were known as the Three Guarantees. The plan had nothing but kind words for Spain and Spaniards and the legacy they bequeathed to Mexico. Although Spain would withhold official recognition of Mexican independence for another fifteen years, its representative on the scene, Superior Political Chief Juan O'Donojú, signed a treaty recognizing Mexico's independence on August 24, 1821, and from that point onward independence was an accomplished fact. On September 27 Iturbide and his army made their triumphal entry into Mexico City amid artillery salvos, ringing church bells, fireworks, flower petals, and the Te Deum played by several orchestras.

According to the Plan of Iguala, government power was to be exercised for the time being by a junta, or committee, of notable men who would assemble the new congress. Of the thirty-eight men Iturbide named to the Junta, not a single one had fought in or sympathized with the rebel armies, and none advocated republicanism. On September 28 this Junta issued an Act of Independence of the Mexican Empire that was effusive in its praise for Iturbide but said not a word about the eleven-year struggle for independence that had preceded his belated "revolution." Clearly, the men who were now setting themselves up to exercise power in the new nation were not the ones who had fought for independence, and most had in fact been frank enemies of the liberating movement. One would not require extraordinary powers of clairvoyance to see that this simple fact foreshadowed enormous political problems in the offing.

The soldiers who had fought for independence—for the most part, impoverished Indians and castas—were, it seemed, to be shut out of the new nation's ruling class. Worse yet, the high level of provincial independence that had prevailed during the colonial period had been exacerbated by the violent, decade-long independence struggle, and several regions in the new republic were strenuously disinclined to cooperate with any central government. From the outset, calls for federalism—the division of political power among the country's many regions—were strong and insistent. Governing Mexico, then, would require coming to grips with formidable regional, class, and ethnic divisions. It would be a daunting task.

In the United States the generation that secured independence from Britain may have had its disagreements, but those disagreements were not nearly as fundamental as the ones that beset their counterparts in Mexico. Tellingly, during Mexico's first years as an independent republic a full-throated debate erupted regarding who should properly be recognized as the true author of independence. Should that accolade go to Father Hidalgo and his successor Morelos, who had called for popular government, an end to racism, redistribution of wealth, and judicial reforms—revolutionary changes aiming to resolve the country's severe divisions? Or should it go to Iturbide, who sought to appeal to people on every side of the great social divide, in effect denying the very existence of that divide? In any event, the divisions that Hidalgo and Morelos had sought to heal could not be denied for long. Mexico's internal conflicts would soon render it vulnerable to the expansionist whims of its powerful neighbor to the north.

2

THINGS FALL APART

An accident of fate and European power politics had cast the United States and Mexico as neighbors; the United States' determination to increase its national territory set the two countries on a collision course. The collision was not inevitable; nor was its outcome foreordained. Mexico's leaders at the time of independence were in fact quite optimistic, seeing no reason why they should not match the United States' progress in short order. They were confident that their country boasted a great wealth of resources—resources that Spain had perversely failed to develop even while jealously shielding them from the rest of the world.

Unfortunately, Mexico too failed to fully develop its fabled resources, inspiring frustration in Mexico and cupidity in its neighbor to the north. That frustration and cupidity grew exponentially as Mexico grew steadily weaker and more divided. U.S. policymakers, meanwhile, did their bit to exacerbate and take advantage of Mexico's many problems. These trends were already abundantly evident before Mexico completed its first decade of independent life, and they would cost the country dearly in its eventual showdown with the United States.

A ROCKY START:
CENTRALISM VERSUS FEDERALISM

Mexico's beginnings as an independent nation were in many ways inauspicious, though the true extent of its problems would not become apparent for some time. It was, however, clear from the outset that Mexicans had profound disagreements about the kind of government they wished to have and about what social group should wield power.

Agustín de Iturbide's declaration of independence from Spain prescribed a constitutional monarchy for Mexico. Enthusiasts for the institution of monarchy hoped that the king of Spain, Ferdinand VII, or some other member of the Spanish Bourbon line might assume the throne of Mexico, giving the monarchy a clear claim to legitimacy. But Spain refused to recognize Mexico's independence—in fact, it did not recognize Mexico until 1836—and made it clear that no Bourbon prince would consider Mexico's request. Spain's obstinacy engendered much hostility in Mexico and inspired some to argue that Mexico should choose its new ruler from among its own sons. The most vocal and insistent faction hoped to elevate Iturbide himself to Mexico's throne. When soldiers and mobs ransacked the streets and shouted from the galleries of congress in favor of an Iturbide kingship, opponents of the idea—and there were many—stood down. So it was that on May 19, 1822, Agustín de Iturbide was declared Emperor Agustín I. On July 21 he was crowned in a lavish and expensive ceremony.

Agustín I had little time to enjoy his throne. Some in congress tried to place strict limits on his power, and the emperor resisted their efforts. When some congressmen took to conspiring against him, Iturbide responded by dissolving congress. In December 1822 a young army officer named Antonio López de Santa Anna, who headed the battalion of the crucial port city of Veracruz, declared his forces in rebellion against the emperor. In February the army battalion that had been charged with putting down Santa Anna's rebellion instead joined that rebellion. At the end of March, less than a year after his coronation, Iturbide abdicated his throne and sailed off into exile.

In nineteenth-century Mexico, the sine qua non for any rebellion was the "plan"—usually a stirring statement of the principles that a given rebellion claimed to champion. The plan for the anti-Iturbide rebellion, known as the Plan of Casa Mata, demanded popular sovereignty and the reinstallation of congress. Its appeal was principally to people in Mexico's regions and to a powerful segment of the Mexican political class who called themselves variously "federalists," "republicans," or "liberals." A key issue for such people was home rule. During the waning years of the Spanish colony, regional autonomy had increased, and the anarchic wars of independence had accelerated the trend. By the 1820s many of Mexico's regions were ill disposed to take orders from Mexico City, which in their view had scant understanding of or sympathy for their problems and prospects. They often had a point: given the dearth of good roads, a simple exchange of letters between Mexico City and a provincial city some three hundred miles away could easily take three weeks, making central coordination difficult and making regional autonomy a de facto reality regardless of what anyone might wish. Some of the regions that most ardently desired regional autonomy did so largely because they experienced considerable prosperity during the early decades after independence and were reluctant to share that prosperity with a profligate central regime. The state of Zacatecas, for example, had rich silver mines that were not significantly damaged during the war for independence, and with the help of British investors, they quickly came to exceed the best production levels of the colonial period. With a healthy treasury the Zacatecans were able to experiment with bold reforms in education, agriculture, and politics, and they had good reason to suppose that meddling by Mexico City would only diminish their prospects.

Liberals also hoped to do away once and for all with the detritus of medievalism that they associated with the vanquished Spanish colony, and to embrace modernity zealously. They ardently championed Enlightenment ideals—popular sovereignty, individual rights and freedoms, secular government, and legal and social equality. For them, the heroes of independence were men like Miguel Hidalgo, José María Morelos, and Vicente Guerrero—men who, with their dark-skinned, impoverished armies, had fought a desperate struggle to change the very structure of power and wealth in Mexico.

On the other side of the political chasm were the conservatives, who wanted the lion's share of power and control to remain in Mexico City, where it had been since the days of the Aztec Empire. They also wanted power to remain in the hands of the social classes who had wielded it for three hundred years—white men who were born to distinction and authority, the hombres de bien. They wanted to preserve and elevate the institutions that, in their view, had undergirded the glorious Spanish Empire: a strong army, the Catholic Church, and a legitimate monarchy.

Over the years these two sides would adopt different titles for themselves; they would adjust their priorities with circumstances; their power would wax and wane; and they would fall out bitterly among themselves. But their essential disagreements were apparent at the outset of the Mexican Republic, and they proved poisonous and irreparable.

With Iturbide's overthrow, the federalist faction was

greatly encouraged and at least momentarily in charge. The Iturbide interlude had done much to render conservatives weak, disorganized, and on the defensive. The federalists wasted no time in seeking to eradicate the now-defunct empire from memory: they freed political prisoners, replaced the emperor's likeness on the coinage with that of an eagle, canceled planned palace renovations, and nullified the Treaty of Córdoba and the Plan of Iguala, the documents that had set the stage for Iturbide's brief reign. Finally, and most importantly, they declared that Mexico was now free to adopt whatever form of government best suited it. It was a heady moment. In the view of freshly empowered federalists, the country was starting with a clean slate, unencumbered by history or tradition or inherited prejudice, limited only by its leaders' powers to imagine. Those leaders harbored a deep antipathy to the institution of monarchy. "Liberty," whatever precisely that might mean, was the watchword of the hour.

The deputies appointed a provisional executive triumvirate and set to discussing the details of the new government. Somewhat surprisingly, they decided not to dissolve the old congress or to hold new elections, even though the old congress had been elected using a deeply flawed method of deciding representation: instead of being elected according to region and population, representatives were chosen to represent corporate groups (the clergy, the army, and the legal profession). The decision not to convoke elections for a more truly representative legislature provoked a response that was an early harbinger of later woes: political leaders in the states of Jalisco and Zacatecas announced that only a federal republic would suit them, and that they were not bound to obey the national congress or executive power. Other provinces soon seconded that demand. In July the central government sent a fully equipped military expedition to invade Jalisco, but the crisis was resolved through negotiations, which ended in assurances that the regions would indeed have considerable autonomy. This was a full-fledged revolt of the provinces, wherein Mexico's regions made it clear that they fully intended to exercise veto power over any decisions of the central government that were not to their liking.

The most conspicuous fruit of the federalist revolt was the federalist Constitution of 1824, a vital document during the decades preceding Mexico's war with the United States. That constitution divided Mexico into nineteen states and four territories. The territories were to be administered directly by the federal government, while the states were to be "independent, free, and sovereign," with the power to form their own constitutions, legislatures, and state militias. State militias were originally designed to provide for local defense and to escort prisoners and treasury shipments in cases where the regular army was unavailable. They would shortly emerge, however, as the chief stronghold of stubborn federalists, as they were wholly under the control of state governors and in some cases seemed to be little more than the private armies of local warlords. The constitution had other defects as well. It gave congress clear power over the executive, and it failed to create an independent judiciary. It therefore lacked "checks and balances" that might have smoothed the process of power sharing. The constitution also maintained religious intolerance and upheld the traditional exemption from civil law for the clergy and military. Voting for president was to be indirect, based on the decisions of the state legislatures. The president would be the man who garnered the most votes, while the vice president would be the man with the second largest number, which meant that the two heads of the executive branch might well be bitter enemies. In the event, the first presidential election under the new constitution resulted in a victory for General Guadalupe Victoria, a hero of the independence wars, with the vice presidency going to Nicolás Bravo, also an old independence fighter but one of a far more conservative turn of mind.

For all its shortcomings, the 1824 Constitution was a creative response to the tremendous diversity of Mexico. It aimed at institutionalizing the sort of unity within diversity that many thinkers held to be Mexico's best hope. It (theoretically at least) erased distinctions of caste and class, allowing unrestricted male suffrage.

While the constitution was clearly federalist, there was no shortage of critics who warned of the dangers of federalism run amok. One deputy to the constituent congress, liberal Dominican theologian Fray Servando Teresa de Mier—a towering figure in Mexico's independence struggles—rose to denounce the excesses of federalism, which he considered to be overly derivative of foreign models and unsuited to Mexican realities. Federalism, he declared, might work in the United States, as the Anglo-Americans were "a new people, homogeneous, industrious, diligent, enlightened and full of social virtues, educated as a free nation." Mier's view of Mexicans was unflattering: they were, he said, "an old people, heterogeneous, without industry, hostile to work, who wish to live off public office like the Spaniards, as ignorant in the general mass as our fathers, and rotten with the vices that derive from the slavery of three centuries."[1] Federalism, he said, would pave the way for the tyranny of uneducated and irresponsible mobs. He attended the constitutional signing ceremony dressed in black, declaring he was attending the funeral of his country. The other signers were, however, jubilant.

"MANIFEST DESTINY" AND THE MEXICAN FRONTIER

What critics of federalism feared most was, quite simply, the dismemberment of Mexico. It was unquestionably a valid concern, for even the country's core regions had tremendous heterogeneity and a decided lack of national sentiment. Of still greater concern was the fact that more than a quarter of the land that Mexico claimed was largely unsettled. Most of that unsettled land was in Mexico's northern frontier regions, where threats to Mexico's claims were palpable: the Russians made plain their interest in acquiring California, whose inhabitants were nearly all impoverished Indians and where Mexico's presence amounted to only a handful of crumbling missions. The entire northern territory was populated by nomadic tribes who would never willingly accept Mexican rule. Most alarming of all was the presence, to the east, of the United States, whose aggressive expansionist ideology—the ingredients of what would eventually come to be known as Manifest Destiny—was abundantly evident.

In its earliest incarnation the concept of Manifest Destiny was religious, conceived by pilgrims arriving on American shores in search of freedom to practice their exacting brand of Protestant Christianity. As they saw it, they were God's chosen people, led by their deity to a promised land, a virgin land uncorrupted by the taints of Old World politics and the heresies of Roman Catholicism. With the Enlightenment, the religious elements largely gave way to convictions about the rightness of republicanism, democracy, and social equality, but the notion of destiny lost none of its missionary zeal. The concept was protean enough to take on new characteristics as the republic evolved, but in its essence Manifest Destiny said that the Anglo-Saxon peoples of America had the right and indeed the duty to spread the blessings of freedom and civilization to those who dwelled in darkness. This notion was perhaps best expressed by Illinois congressman John Wentworth on the eve of the war with Mexico, who said he "did not believe that the God of Heaven, when he crowned the American arms with success [in the Revolutionary War], designed that the original States should be the only abode of liberty on earth. On the contrary, he only designed them as the great center from which civilization, religion, and liberty should radiate and radiate until the whole continent shall bask in their blessing."[2]

Contradictions, inconsistencies, and much outright hypocrisy were all bound up with the Anglo-Americans' insistence that they had the right to expand their borders. Racial hubris was a large part of the concept: Anglo-Saxons, in this view, were a vibrant and vigorous people, and other races were effeminate, decrepit, and corrupt. Thomas Jefferson, one of the earliest and greatest architects of U.S. expansion, wrote in 1786 that the United States "must be viewed as the nest, from which all America, North and South, is to be peopled." Hardly eager to see the colonies of Spanish America attain their freedom, he rather hoped they would remain in the decrepit hands of the Spanish Empire "till our population can be sufficiently advanced to gain it from them, piece by piece."[3] While theoretically a key goal of American expansion was to redeem backward peoples, few of the architects of American expansion were optimistic regarding the prospects for redeeming the peoples of Latin America. Jefferson was convinced that free government and Roman Catholicism were simply incompatible. John Quincy Adams denounced Spanish Americans as "the most ignorant, the most bigoted, the most superstitious of all the Roman Catholics in Christendom" and insisted that to try to convert them to true democracy would be "as absurd as similar plans would be to establish democracies among the birds, beasts, and fishes."[4]

The issue of race underlay the notion of Manifest Destiny in other, still more insidious ways. Defenders of slavery, mostly concentrated in the southern states, believed that the lands south of the Mexican border were in some ways uniquely hospitable to human bondage, and that those lands held the key to the preservation of that "peculiar institution." By expanding southward, slave owners hoped to increase their representation within the Union. Ironically, opponents of slavery also found reason for southward expansion. Thomas Jefferson, though himself a slave owner, was convinced that slavery's days were numbered, but he was equally convinced that the white and black races were profoundly unequal and would be unable to live side by side in peace. Free blacks would have to be sent off to colonize some foreign place. Jefferson favored the West Indies for this purpose. Others felt that just about any territory to the south would make an excellent dumping ground for freed blacks, which would in turn preserve the racial uniformity of the United States and hence its peace and security.

Whatever the reasons or justifications, the United States embarked on its expansionist career very early on in its history. For the most part that expansion was remarkably peaceful, accomplished through purchase and negotiation— supplemented by the occasional bit of trickery—rather than through military exploits. In 1803 the United States reaped a windfall when France sold it the Louisiana Territory, an enormous swath of land stretching from New Orleans in the South westward to the northern Rockies and east to the Mississippi River. The boundaries included in that transaction were vague, leading the United States to claim that both West Florida (which stretched between the Apalachicola and Mississippi Rivers) and Texas were included in it. By 1812 the United States had managed to assert its claim to West Florida. The boundary between Louisiana and Texas, however, remained in dispute: Spain claimed that Louisiana ended around Natchitoches, while the United States suggested that it ran to the Rio Grande.

Meanwhile American adventurers, with tacit endorsement from Washington, continued to encroach on East Florida, which was regarded as essential to U.S. security. After 1810 Spain, while fighting desperate wars to retain its wealthy colonies in Mexico and South America, felt it hardly worth the effort to defend East Florida, a relatively undeveloped frontier region. When forces led by Andrew Jackson invaded and occupied the territory in 1818, the United States, in effect, dared Spain to do something about it. Spain decided to negotiate.

The fruit of these negotiations was the Adams-Onís Treaty, concluded in 1819. Under the terms of the treaty, Spain sold Florida to the United States and agreed to abandon all claims to lands in the Pacific Northwest, in exchange for a U.S. pledge to renounce its claim to Texas and to forgive $5 million worth of unpaid claims owed to U.S. citizens. The treaty set the boundary line at the Sabine River, the boundary between the modern states of Louisiana and Texas.

Though not apparent at the time, the Adams-Onís Treaty was a key development leading to the U.S.-Mexican War. The Mexicans, who inherited the treaty upon attaining their independence from Spain, maintained that it made their claim to Texas legally unassailable. Many Americans, for their part, heatedly denounced the treaty and its architect, Secretary of State John Quincy Adams. In their view, Texas was clearly part of the Louisiana Purchase, and signing away the U.S. claim to it was positively treasonous. Those who were convinced that Texas was rightfully part of the United States were not easily dissuaded. Anglo-Americans had been mounting armed expeditions into the region since 1801. Incensed by the Adams-Onís Treaty, Dr. James Long, a friend of Andrew Jackson, invaded Texas in the summer of 1819 with a small band of armed adventurers in hopes of claiming the territory for the United States, but the expedition was ill-fated and eventually cost Dr. Long his life.

Dr. Long's failure ended the age of the filibusters, as private armies were known (the term *filibuster* is derived from *freebooter*, or pirate). Such expeditions were manned mostly by roguish adventurers, and their actions were illegal by nearly any reckoning. But the end of filibustering also marked the start of a new epoch in the history of Texas, for the Mexican government had determined that bold measures would have to be tried if Mexico's northern regions were to be retained.

The Mexicans were keenly aware of how vulnerable those regions were. While no codified international law existed on the issue, there was a general understanding among nations that a country's claim to a given territory would remain tenuous unless and until that country could establish significant settlement on the land in question, building cities and infrastructure and otherwise cementing its ownership. That was precisely what the Mexicans realized they must do. But there was a sticking point: where precisely were the colonists to come from? Mexico's own population was sparse. The vast region from Oregon to Guatemala held fewer than seven million inhabitants, many of them peasants with deep ties to the land and no incentive to move to an unsettled land filled with hostile Indians. Dimming the colonization prospects further, many Mexican officials took a dim view of their own compatriots, insisting that the "Mexican character" was poorly suited to colonization. Clearly, if Mexicans were unable, unwilling, or unsuited to colonize the northern regions, then foreigners would have to be enticed to do the job. Anglo-Americans were eager to oblige, but from the Mexican point of view, relying on such immigrants would be perilous. The Mexicans had seen how American migration into West and East Florida had proved a prelude to U.S. seizure of those lands from Spain. Indeed, the Americans were fairly open in viewing their migrants as the advance guard of empire. When Spain had opened its Louisiana Territory to foreign immigrants in 1788, Thomas Jefferson wrote that he wished "a hundred thousand of our inhabitants would accept the invitation. It may be the means of delivering to us peaceably what may otherwise cost us a war."[5]

The Spanish government had done its best to prohibit migration from the United States into Texas, though Americans did indeed settle there as squatters. The government of independent Mexico generally shared Spain's view of Anglo-Americans, which held that they were unassimilable, subversive, and untrustworthy. Even so, the matter of colonizing Texas was pressing: only settlement could secure Mexico's claim to Texas, and Texas must be secured to serve as a buffer against U.S. expansion. It was a wicked conundrum, but accepting Anglo-American immigrants appeared to be the only recourse. Mexican officials consoled themselves with the thought that Anglo-Americans were skilled and diligent, and once they had tamed Texas, it might be a more attractive destination for migrants from other countries, including Mexico itself. Eventually, they hoped, a balance might be achieved.

In 1819 a man named Moses Austin, a New Englander who had made and lost a fortune mining lead in Missouri, traveled to Texas and solicited permission to start an Anglo-American colony there. After some initial hesitation, Texas governor Antonio Martínez granted him permission. The trip to and from Texas was so strenuous, however, that Moses Austin's health was irreparably ruined, and he died in the summer of 1821. His dying wish was that his son should take up his colonization project where he left off, and Stephen—then twenty-eight years old—proved more than equal to the task.

Stephen F. Austin was of a decidedly different breed from the rough-and-tumble filibusters who had tried since 1801 to take Texas by force. He was likable, handsome, hardworking, and well educated, with cultivated manners, a moderate temperament, and a sometimes unfortunate tendency to assume the good intentions of others. He arrived in Texas in June 1821, even as his father was dying in Missouri and as Mexico was in the process of securing its independence from Spain. During the Spanish period Texas had been a remote frontier region where intrepid missionaries sought to evangelize recalcitrant Indians. The scene of a savage military campaign during Mexico's war of independence, its Spanish-speaking population had been reduced from a high of some four thousand in 1810 to barely more than two thousand in 1820, most of them concentrated in the dilapidated villages of San Antonio de Béxar and La Bahia (soon to be renamed Goliad, an anagram for Hidalgo, the hero of independence). The *tejanos* (as Mexican residents of Texas were called) kept some cattle and horses and raised a bit of corn, but it was the extremes of their poverty that most impressed Stephen Austin—they had, he reported, "little furniture or rather none at all in their houses—no knives, eat with forks and spoons and their fingers."[6] The province was also home to perhaps forty thousand Indians belonging to at least thirty-one tribes, many of whom were nomadic warriors— Comanches, Caddos, Kiowas, Karankawas, and others.

Austin's petition to have his father's colonization project reaffirmed was approved by Governor Martínez, and he began bringing in migrants. But in such uncertain times, there was doubt as to who had the authority to approve Austin's contract, and it became clear that his only hope of starting a legal settlement was to travel to Mexico City. Austin thus, from the outset, made plain his intention to do everything by the book, and for most of his adult life he never wavered from his commitment to be a good citizen of Mexico.

Austin arrived in Mexico City in early May 1822. There was no doubting his resolve: he diligently studied the Spanish language, eagerly solicited Mexican citizenship, and cultivated good relations with Mexican statesmen—especially those who served on the congressional colonization committee, which was in the process of writing Mexico's colonization law. Although Austin had near-superhuman patience and a remarkable ability to befriend men of all ideological persuasions, he was fairly appalled by the political intrigues of the Mexican capital. Such intrigues stretched what he had assumed would be a perfunctory trip of two weeks into an ordeal of eleven months.

The colonization committee drew up a colonization law and sent it to congress for debate within a month of the Emperor Iturbide's coronation. Although some details would change, this bill served as the model for all that followed. The law said that land would be distributed to *empresarios*, who would contract to bring in at least two hundred families to settle in the frontier regions. Settlers who were not already Roman Catholic would be required to adopt that faith, and the government would be bound to protect their property, freedom, and civil rights. To further induce settlement, settlers would be exempt from all taxation during their first six years in the country, and goods imported for use by the colonists were partially tax exempt. The children of slaves brought into Mexican territory would be free at the age of fourteen, and the slave trade was prohibited. A head of family was entitled to 4,438 acres of land for farming and an additional 177 acres if he planned to raise livestock. Empresarios would be awarded 66,774 acres for every two hundred immigrants they brought in. It was a remarkably generous law, with land grants twice as large as Austin had initially asked for.

The passage of the law was long delayed by Iturbide's dissolution of congress in October, and by the rebellion that erupted against his regime in December. The emperor finally signed the law on January 4, 1823. It was annulled along with all other Iturbide-era legislation upon his overthrow in March, but in August 1824 another, nearly identical, colonization law replaced it. Austin's own empresario contract was approved by congress in early April, and he returned to Texas, a bit chastened and more cynical than he had been a year earlier. "They are a strange people," he wrote of the Mexicans, "and must be studied to be managed." Austin held that the Mexicans made much of their national honor but would cheerfully betray that honor if they could do so without being exposed. Ever the good citizen, however, he sternly admonished his colonists in Texas "not to meddle with politics, and to have nothing to do with any revolutionary schemes."[7]

Austin, who soon negotiated two additional colonization contracts, was by far the most successful of several empresarios, who settled large numbers of American families in the state. Adding to these numbers were many Americans who migrated into Texas illegally. Soon Anglo-Americans became the overwhelmingly dominant element in the Texas population. Most of them had no intention of abiding by their end of the bargain.

POLITICS AND POINSETT

As the Anglo-American colonies began to grow and flourish, Mexican officials became increasingly uneasy about U.S. intentions toward Texas. U.S. newspapers, complained Mexican chargé d'affaires Manuel Zozaya in 1823, routinely sang the praises of Texas and suggested that it rightfully belonged to the United States. Political opponents of John Quincy Adams, Zozaya reported, made the former secretary of state's role in signing away U.S. claims to Texas a major political issue in the 1824 presidential campaign, in which Adams was the leading contender. The secretary of the Mexican legation at Washington, Colonel José Anastasio Torrens, added further to Mexican anxieties when he recounted a conversation he had had with General Andrew Jackson. Jackson, the most dynamic political force in the country, allegedly explained to Torrens that the best way to gain territory was to occupy it and, after effective possession was gained in that fashion, to "treat for it." That, he said, was how the United States got possession of the Floridas, an affair in which Jackson himself had played a leading role. Torrens and other diplomats also complained of American haughtiness, for many American politicos were brazenly contemptuous of Mexicans and disdained Mexican claims. Torrens and others warned against allowing Anglo-Americans to become predominant in Texas, even as Stephen F. Austin was consolidating his colony there.

Adding still further to Mexican anxiety was the appointment in 1825 of the first U.S. ambassador to Mexico, one Joel Roberts Poinsett. A former high-ranking official of the Iturbide government claimed that during an 1822 visit to Mexico, Poinsett had unfurled a map of North America and, pointing to the boundary specified in the treaty of 1819, declared it "undesirable." The United States, Poinsett had casually explained, wanted Texas, New Mexico, and Upper California, as well as parts of Lower California, Sonora, Coahuila, and Nuevo León. It was no great leap for Mexicans to assume that Poinsett was the advance guard of American avarice.

Poinsett is best remembered in the United States for his signal accomplishment as an amateur botanist—it was he who introduced into the United States the Mexican Flor de la Noche Buena (Christmas Eve Flower), which became the poinsettia. In Mexico, however, he is best remembered for meddling.

A native of Charleston, South Carolina, Poinsett was an intrepid traveler whose colorful résumé included time spent in the court of Czar Alexander I of Russia at the height of the Napoleonic Wars, where he declined an offer of a colonelcy in the czar's army. He traveled extensively in Europe and the Middle East, everywhere finding that the rest of the world came up grievously short in comparison with his own beloved country. "It is impossible," he once wrote, "for me to speak of my country otherwise than with fondest partiality—a country which Liberty, leaving the nations of Europe to mourn her flight in the gloom of despotism and corruption, has chosen as her favorite asylum. Long may her bright influence extend over my happy country. Long may she enlighten a grateful people who . . . cherish her with the warmest enthusiasm."[8]

Touching as Poinsett's enthusiasm may have been, it also made him in some ways a singularly poor choice for the position of U.S. ambassador to Mexico. Poinsett's love of his country blinded him to its deficiencies and hypocrisies and ensured that he would take a jaundiced view of any foreigners who did not aspire to imitate the Anglo-Americans. Himself a slave owner, he was only moderately troubled by the obvious fact that liberty had bestowed its blessings selectively. Like all enlightened republicans, he professed to believe that nations should possess the right to determine their own course; yet at the same time he derided any system that did not closely resemble that of the United States, and he was seldom bashful or apologetic about nudging things in that direction. During the 1810s the U.S. government sent him to South America with orders to cultivate good relations and trading contacts between the United States and the South American countries. Instructed to maintain strict neutrality, Poinsett instead fraternized openly with liberal independence fighters in Chile, even helpfully offering them his own draft constitution, modeled closely on that of the United States.

In 1822 the U.S. government sent Poinsett—by now quite fluent in Spanish and a putative authority on Latin American culture—to Mexico to report on conditions there. His report, published in 1824, painted a mixed portrait of Mexico. Poinsett, like Austin, was appalled by the extremes of poverty and inequality he witnessed, put off by the excessive religiosity of Mexican Catholicism, and scandalized by the drunkenness, cockfights, tobacco-smoking women, beggars, and bandits, as well as the squat mud huts of the common people ("I certainly never saw a negro house in Carolina so comfortless.") Above all Poinsett despised the Emperor Iturbide, for Iturbide represented the loathsome Old World practices of monarchism and autocracy. He steadfastly believed that the majority of the Mexican people clamored for republicanism as practiced in the United States of America.

Poinsett lost little time in alienating a significant portion of Mexico's ruling class. The problems were partly caused by international rivalry. Great Britain, eager to partake of Mexico's fabled wealth, sent as its chargé d'affaires one Henry George Ward, who sought advantage for England partly by discrediting the American ambassador at every opportunity. Ward made a point of placing Poinsett's every indiscreet utterance before the Mexican president and press, hoping to inflame prejudice against him. The two diplomats would give banquets for Mexican politicians, each always pointedly not inviting the other and each gleefully excoriating his rival during the customary banquet orations.

Poinsett's official instructions caused problems, for they urged discretion but not impartiality. He was "to show on all occasions an unobtrusive readiness to explain the practical operation and the very great advantages which appertain to our system." More damaging, he was instructed to open a dialogue on three sensitive topics: the independence of Cuba, which the United States opposed and which the Mexicans favored; preferential treatment for U.S. commerce; and most controversial of all, the possession of Texas.

Poinsett was instructed to try to persuade the Mexicans to part with Texas. Those instructions, authored by Secretary of State Henry Clay, said Poinsett should push for a boundary as far to the west as possible, preferably the Rio Grande. Failing that, he should argue that the boundary be either the Colorado or the Brazos River. The case that Clay suggested Poinsett make to Mexican officials was not only unpersuasive, it was insulting. Clay argued that by ceding Texas, Mexico would save much money, for it would be relieved of the burden of fighting the Comanches and other warlike Indians. He also suggested that, as the population of Texas expanded, friction would increase over the navigation of shared river systems, which could easily be obviated by Mexico's relinquishing territory. Finally, severing the northern half of Mexico's territory would bring the blessing of placing Mexico's capital city in a more central location within the country (this from the representative of a country whose capital was on the mid-Atlantic seaboard, some sixteen hundred miles from San Antonio). The case was so absurd, and Mexican feelings on the issue so raw, that Poinsett, diplomatically and in code, declined to follow his instructions, suggesting to Clay that the matter was best left to fate. "Most of the good land from the Colorado to the Sabine," he advised, "has been granted by the state of Texas and is rapidly peopling with either grantees or squatters from the United States, a population [the Mexicans] will find difficult to govern, and perhaps after a short period they may not be so averse to part with that portion of their territory as they are at present."[9] This, of course, was precisely the strategy that Andrew Jackson had outlined to Colonel Torrens.

In fact, Poinsett was extremely discreet regarding Texas, generally ignoring requests from the American administration to raise the issue on the grounds that the administration simply did not understand the intensity of Mexican feelings on the matter. He was less discreet in one of his early and most notorious forays into Mexican politics, which involved the founding of a Masonic lodge.

In 1825, when Poinsett arrived in Mexico, Freemasonry was already well established there. The first lodges established in Mexico pertained to the Scottish rite, which some critics charged with being overly favorable toward monarchy, aristocracy, and the church. In order to counter their influence, Mexican liberals wished to organize lodges of the York rite, which would advocate federalism, republicanism, anticlericalism, and expanded suffrage. Poinsett, himself a great champion of those values, helped to organize the first York rite lodge, holding meetings for a time in his own home and securing the society's charter from the grand lodge of New York.

The rivalry between the Yorkinos and Escoceses, as the two groups were known, quickly grew bitter and heated. A more poisonous prescription for the new nation's politics could hardly have been devised, for the rival lodges operated as closed, secret societies. In the highly charged political environment of early republican Mexico, and in the absence of established political parties or nonpartisan press organs, the Masonic lodges came to operate much like rival gangs, devoting themselves to intrigue and assuming that their enemies were engaged in the most vicious conspiracies and subterfuges. During the second half of the 1820s the Yorkinos steadily gained power and influence throughout the republic—and with it the enmity of the Escoces faction. Conservative antipathy toward Poinsett increased in proportion to Yorkino power, and despite his public statements that he regretted the politicization of the societies and had ceased contact with them once their political nature became clear, conservatives came to see him as the very inventor of Mexico's political discord.

Each of the two antagonistic lodges founded its own newspaper, and journalism became a blood sport. Since neither side had accurate information about what the other was up to, they gave their imaginations free rein. The Escoceses were alarmed that the Yorkinos deliberately curried support among the underclass—those they derided as the "sans-culottes," the rabble—the people who had run amok during the revolution for independence, who loathed whites, and who threatened to snuff out the light of civilization. This activity was especially terrifying because the Yorkinos were unselective in their recruiting, so that to the Escoceses their numbers appeared to be increasing like a ghastly pestilence. The Escoceses feared that the Yorkinos, with their zealous embrace of federalism, intended to hoard all funds at the local level, bleeding the national treasury dry. The Yorkinos, for their part, suspected that the Escoceses were conspiring with Spanish monarchists to turn the clock back to the darkest days of the colonies, taking away the hard-won liberties of the provinces and the lower classes.

The Yorkinos' most reckless and damaging initiative was a demagogic campaign against the country's Spaniards. Spain fueled passions by obstinately refusing to acknowledge Mexico's independence and threatening a reconquest. Yorkinos tended to associate Spain with the racial hierarchy that had oppressed and exploited the country's Indians and mestizos for three centuries. They also claimed, with some justice, that Spaniards still held a disproportionate share of the nation's wealth and political power.

The Yorkinos' xenophobia took an ugly turn in 1827. In January of that year a middle-aged Spanish-born monk named Joaquín Arenas, a specialist in the production of counterfeit money, was arrested and charged with conspiring to return Mexico to Spanish rule. Soon some thirty-five other alleged co-conspirators, including a pair of distinguished generals, were taken into custody. The plot seems largely to have been a figment of the Yorkinos' paranoid imagination, but nevertheless the Yorkino papers were soon buzzing with a near-hysterical debate on what should be the republic's attitude toward Spain and Spaniards. The Yorkinos charged that the Escoceses were part of the monarchist conspiracy, and the Escoceses countered that the conspiracy charges were merely another stunt in the ongoing Yorkino power grab. In December, after a spate of anti-Spanish riots and vigilante violence throughout the country, the Yorkino-controlled congress passed a bill giving Spaniards six months to leave the country.

Conservatives saw in all of this further evidence of what they most feared: the ignorant rabble were bent on nothing less than the destruction of civilization. Vice President Nicolás Bravo, grand master of the Escoceses, headed a rebellion in December 1827. The rebels demanded that all secret societies be banned, certain government ministers be purged, and the constitution be respected. Yielding nothing to the Yorkinos in their proclivity for demogogic scapegoating, they also demanded that Ambassador Joel Poinsett be expelled from the country. By this time conservative Mexicans were convinced that Poinsett, by injecting pernicious alien ideas into the nation's bloodstream, was the person primarily responsible for setting Mexico on a ruinous path. They saw his actions as part of a deliberate U.S. plot to weaken Mexico, setting it up for eventual dismemberment. State legislatures demanded Poinsett's expulsion, riots erupted, and he received death threats.

Vice President Bravo's rebellion lasted only about two weeks before being defeated by the forces of General Vicente Guerrero. Although this rebellion was unsuccessful, it was enormously important in establishing a tragic precedent: it signaled a wholesale loss of faith in the rule of law and a willingness to embrace violence as a means of gaining political ends.

The defeat of the conservatives brought not peace but rather further complication and enmity. A group of liberals, frightened by the increase in radicalism, had bolted the Yorkinos and founded a faction of Impartials that backed the fairly nondescript Manuel Gómez Pedraza for the presidency in 1828. The radical Yorkinos favored Vicente Guerrero, a hero of the independence wars. Guerrero was a former muleteer of mixed Indian, black, and white race for whom Spanish was a second language.

It was a vicious campaign, but after all the mudslinging and voting was over, Gómez Pedraza claimed a majority of votes. Guerrero's supporters immediately resorted to rebellion, beginning with an uprising in the state of Veracruz, headed by General Antonio López de Santa Anna, that demanded that Gómez Pedraza's election be nullified and that there be another round of expulsions of Spaniards. The rebellion seemed to be sputtering when it was joined at the end of November by a garrison within Mexico City, which launched an attack from an old prison-turned-armory known as the Acordada. Soon Gómez Pedraza fled into exile, and Vicente Guerrero assumed the presidency.

The most memorable event of this so-called Rebellion of the Acordada took place on December 4 and 5, when rebel soldiers, joined by beggars and escaped prisoners, attacked a complex of shops known as El Parián on Mexico City's posh central square. The rebels justified their attack by claiming that most of the shops were owned by Spaniards and that their goods could be claimed as spoils of war, though in fact most of the shops were Mexican owned. The violence of the attack was appalling. The attackers plundered some two to three million pesos worth of goods, murdered merchants, stabbed one another, set the shops ablaze, and even looted the storerooms of the National Palace. At least a thousand people were left destitute by the riots. Such a scene, occurring as it did in the city's elegant main square, afforded conservatives the most chilling glimpse yet of the specter of barbarism. Once again they conjured up the old analogies to sans-culottes running amok in the French Revolution. They decided that they would have to redouble their efforts to crush this trend toward unrestrained democracy and concentrate power in their own hands—wealthy, civilized, responsible hands.

By the start of 1829 the optimism of the early Mexican republic was a fading memory. "The country," wrote conservative leader Lucas Alamán, "is consuming and ruining itself at full speed."[10] Mexico's liberals and conservatives made no room for compromise: both factions had come to view politics as an ongoing crisis, and compromise seemed a potentially fatal mistake. Infighting among the factions, and disputes between the center and the regions, helped to ensure that the central

government's finances would remain precarious. The constitution spoke of the equality of all Mexican citizens, but the
distance between rich and poor was vast and increasing. Only
a few years before, many Mexicans had thought that their nation might catch up with or overtake the United States in
power and wealth. Such hopes had long since been abandoned. Although some in the liberal camp continued to regard the United States as a model and an inspiration, their
positive sentiments were fading and resentment was building
steadily. Other Mexicans saw the United States as the source
of a pernicious ideology that was destroying Mexico from
within, paving the way for a treacherous assault on the nation's vulnerable territories.

There was at least one apparent bright spot: in Texas,
Stephen F. Austin's colony was flourishing. He and several
other empresarios had signed contracts to settle more than
eight thousand families in Texas, and Austin was well on his
way to fulfilling his contracts. And Austin, at least, seemed
the ideal empresario, a man who eschewed partisanship and
was emphatically resolved to be a good and loyal citizen of
Mexico. In fact, however, despite Austin's efforts, Texas was
already slipping out of Mexico's grasp.

3

THE PROBLEM OF TEXAS

For a couple of years after the colonization law of 1824 went into effect, officials in Mexico City paid scant attention to Mexico's remote northern provinces, finding plenty of issues much closer to home to stir their political passions and command their full attention. But a series of events in Texas soon converted that troublesome state into nothing less than a national obsession, and that obsession goes far toward explaining why Mexico went to war with the United States.

THE TEXAS BOUNDARY COMMISSION

The Mexicans, of course, had never been comfortable with the prospect of U.S. citizens settling in Texas, and that prospect came to seem increasingly less welcome as more and more Anglo-Americans found their way to Texas. Many of those migrants came illegally, some seeking cheap land and a fresh start, others trying to escape debts contracted in other climes. Still others were fugitives from justice, sporting brands on their faces marking them as miscreants. In 1823, when the first colonization law was written, perhaps three thousand such squatters were already living in Texas. Part of the intent of the colonization law was to regulate the influx of settlers, ensuring that the Texans would be of "good character." But the existence of the colonization law did little to impede the illegal immigration, which greatly supplemented the legal variety. By 1830 the Anglo population exceeded twenty thousand, while the Mexican inhabitants numbered barely over three thousand.

Well aware of this growing imbalance, the British chargé d'affaires in Mexico, H. G. Ward—Ambassador Poinsett's archnemesis—went to some lengths during the 1820s to inflame Mexican anxieties regarding U.S. intentions toward Texas. He reminded the Mexican government that the Adams-Onís Treaty of 1819, wherein the United States had formally renounced its claims to Texas, had never been ratified by independent Mexico, and that the boundary between U.S. and Mexican territory was neither firmly agreed upon nor clearly marked. The Mexicans had long recognized that the 1819 treaty was essential to their retention of Texas, but so far there had been little movement toward solidifying that agreement. Ward urged the Mexican government to send a commission to Texas to determine landmarks for the boundary and, while they were at it, to carry out a close investigation of the colonization efforts.

Political turmoil and penury prevented the Mexican congress from appropriating funds for such an expedition for two years. But then, in early 1827, sobering news arrived: at the end of 1826 an American empresario named Haden Edwards had launched a rebellion aimed at detaching Texas from the Mexican Republic. Edwards, in an alliance with Cherokee Indians who at least momentarily shared Edwards's resentment of the Mexican authorities, planned to call the new nation the Republic of the Red and White People or, alternatively, the

Republic of Fredonia. The rebellion collapsed as soon as a detachment of two hundred Mexican soldiers arrived from San Antonio, supported by another contingent from Stephen F. Austin's colony. Edwards and his supporters fled to the United States, and the rebellion fizzled.

Short-lived though it was, the Fredonian Revolt seemed to confirm the Mexicans' darkest fears regarding the intentions of the Anglo-Americans toward Texas. By coincidence, news of the Fredonian uprising reached Mexico on the very day that Padre Arenas was arrested for conspiring with Spain, adding to a general fear that the country, in its weakened condition, was to be the object of foreign aggression from all directions and that gradual dismemberment was a very real possibility. Compounding that fear, the U.S. government, while disavowing any knowledge of or sympathy for the Fredonian Revolt, sought to exploit Mexican anxieties over the episode by instructing Ambassador Poinsett to offer the Mexicans up to a million dollars for the territory bounded by the Rio Grande, and half that amount for the territory bounded by the Colorado River. Poinsett gingerly broached the topic with Mexican authorities, but once again the reception was so hostile that he quickly abandoned the effort. The U.S. offer, tepid though it was, further persuaded the Mexicans that resolute action on Texas was urgent.

So it was that in 1827 the Mexican congress finally appropriated the funds for a boundary commission to Texas. Chosen to lead the expedition was General Manuel de Mier y Terán, by all accounts one of the most capable and dedicated men in the Mexican army. General Terán had graduated from the Mexican College of Mines in 1811 with a degree in engineering and had put his knowledge and skills to work during the independence war as a member of the rebel forces of José María Morelos. He became administrative director of the National School of Artillery upon its founding in 1824 and the same year was named acting secretary of war and the navy. He was a member of the Scottish rite Masonic lodge and a close friend of Lucas Alamán, the leading conservative of his generation. Although his sentiments and associations indicate a generally conservative disposition, Terán was more patriot than partisan. He was appalled by the factional squabbles that plagued the Mexican Republic. A life of reclusive scientific study would clearly have suited his temperament far better than his actual life in the maelstrom of Mexican politics, and he suffered frequent bouts of what he chose to call "melancholy." He commanded near-unanimous confidence and respect, even while remaining generally taciturn and reserved. One Mexican official described him as "a man of much knowledge, understanding and astuteness, not easy to become friendly with, holds strictly to convention, is formidable with his logic and persuasion, and is of an analytical turn of mind."[1]

The Boundary Commission left Mexico City on November 10, 1827, traveling in an immense coach built from heavy wooden beams that were intricately carved and inlaid with silver. Accompanying Terán were José María Sánchez, a cartographer, and Jean-Louis Berlandier, a French botanist and zoologist, as well as a mineralogist, a geographer, and a medical corpsman. The commission was well supplied with scientific gadgets, as study of the flora, fauna, minerals, climate, and resources was key to the mission. In addition to performing its scientific work, the commission was instructed to survey and mark the Texas-U.S. boundary as delineated in the 1819 treaty; evaluate the number and kinds of troops needed to defend the region; estimate costs; report on the conditions of the current inhabitants; make alliances and secure commercial treaties with the Indians of the region; and recommend measures that might help to ensure Mexico's continued possession of Texas. Terán, Sánchez, and Berlandier all kept copious notes and diaries of the voyage.

Predictably, given the prevailing prejudices of their social class, the commissioners found little to admire in the Mexican inhabitants of Texas, known as *tejanos*. The tejanos were concentrated almost entirely in San Antonio de Béxar, Goliad, and Nacogdoches in the east. San Antonio (better known at the time as Béxar), the most important of these settlements, was a rude village with a total population of 1,425. It was surrounded by Comanche and Tahuacano Indians who kept the settlers under more or less constant siege and prevented much farming, despite the richness of the soil. According to Terán and his colleagues, the tejanos living there were lazy and would have been uninterested in farming in any case. The Mexican troops stationed there—the only defense against hostile Indians and ambitious foreigners—were perpetually undersupplied by the government with even the most basic necessities. That neglect, added to the difficulties of transport and the ever-present threat of Indian attacks that obstructed trade, forced them to subsist on corn cakes ground into barely edible mush, some dry salted beef, and whatever wild game they could kill. Commission cartographer José María Sánchez lamented that the tejanos could barely be considered Mexican, since they spoke Spanish badly and were "ignorant not only of the customs of our great cities, but even of the occurrences of our Revolution."[2]

To be sure, the commissioners' assessment of the tejanos' condition was unduly harsh. In fact, the tejanos were a people quite culturally distinct from the educated and aristocratic commissioners from central Mexico. They had forged a strong sense of community and a communal work ethic akin to that of Mexico's indigenous communities, which were likewise derided by many elite Mexicans. Their culture had developed in part due to their having to provide for and defend themselves, with little assistance from the government at Mexico City. Like other Mexican provincial peoples, they came to expect little of the central government; rather, they came to mistrust it and to resent its intrusions into their affairs. The tejanos became, in short, staunch federalists. The most influential tejanos tended to prefer the liberalism of the Anglo-Americans over the stodgy hierarchies of central Mexico. No doubt they greeted the commissioners coldly.

The commissioners also found Texas's Indian population disappointing. Small nomadic tribes who had lived by hunting deer, bear, ducks, and other game had lapsed into the direst poverty, for many of the state's creatures had been hunted nearly to extinction to satisfy a thriving trade in pelts. Several tribes—the Comanches, Tahuacanos, Lipanes, Wacos, Caihuas—showed not the slightest interest in settling down, assimilating, or ceasing their hostilities toward whites (although they clearly held the Mexicans in higher esteem than the Anglos; while they might kill Mexicans, they would subject Anglos to excruciating torture). Still others—most notably the Karankawas of East Texas—had a history of conflict with the white settlers and by 1828 had nearly all been killed. A number of peaceful sedentary groups inhabited the region around Nacogdoches—the Cherokees, Kickapoos, Delawares, and Alabamas—trading with the Mexicans there. The Mexicans had some hopes for the Cherokees in particular, for although few in number they were "the best of all the Indians," in General Terán's words. If granted secure titles to their lands, the Mexicans hoped, the Cherokees might serve as a useful counterweight to the Anglo-Americans.

The Boundary Commission found much to admire, and much to fear, in the Anglo-American communities. The eastern part of the state, where the Anglo-American settlements were concentrated, was an "enchanted country" where the Guadalupe, Brazos, and Colorado Rivers flowed through dense woodlands and vast plains. In April, when the commission passed through, those plains were bursting with wildflowers. Stephen Austin's colony, centered at the small village of San Felipe de Austin on the banks of the Brazos, consisted of some forty or fifty wooden houses inhabited by perhaps

200 people, only 10 of them Mexicans. Surrounding the village were the farms of some 1,800 settlers and 443 black slaves. The settlers, according to commissioner José María Sánchez, were "independent and haughty," so much so that on the rare occasions when they greeted the commissioners with kindness, it would come as a great and pleasant surprise.

The people of Austin's colony, however, seemed more enterprising and ambitious than their tejano counterparts, though the commissioners disagreed on precisely what that portended. Terán, who liked and admired Stephen F. Austin, wrote that, among the several Anglo-American colonies in Texas, Austin's colony was "the only one where they try to understand and obey the laws of the country and where, as a result of the enlightenment and integrity of its empresario, they have a notion of our republic and its government."[3] Trouble, according to Terán, was more likely to come from other, more unruly colonies and from the many squatters who had settled in Texas illegally. For José María Sánchez, however, Austin's colony was in fact the source of greatest concern. Austin had cultivated a reputation as a consummate diplomat and respectable citizen of Mexico, always taking the side of the Mexican government against malcontents within his colony, nurturing friendships with Mexican authorities, and learning Spanish well enough to compose all his official correspondence in that language. This, according to Sánchez, had "lulled authorities into a sense of security, while he works diligently for his own ends. In my judgment, the spark that will start the conflagration that will deprive us of Texas, will start from this colony."[4]

General Terán was not complacent about the Austin colony, despite the admirable attitude of its empresario. Nearly all of the trade from Austin's colony, he noted, was with the United States. Indeed, the site of the colony had been chosen precisely for its strategic economic advantages: the Brazos and other navigable rivers carried goods to the ports of Matagorda and Galveston, from whence New Orleans was an easy three-day sail across the Gulf of Mexico. Two ships per month arrived at Texas ports from New Orleans, and others from New York and Philadelphia, unloading all manner of luxury goods, tools, and machinery and taking on cotton, livestock products, furs, and other commodities. Mules raised in Austin's colony were sold in the English and French colonies in the Caribbean. At the same time a vigorous overland trade developed connecting the East Texas settlements to the commercial hub of Natchitoches in Louisiana. The pull of commercial interests, combined with the lack of positive acts from Mexico, all tended to bind Texas ever more closely to the United States. The same was true of the New Mexico Territory to the west, which after 1821 did a substantial commerce with the United States over the Santa Fe Trail. While Mexico's economy generally stagnated, its northern states prospered owing entirely to their economic links to the booming U.S. economy. Economically, then, Mexico was practically irrelevant to the Texas colonies except insofar as it collected customs duties and imposed commercial regulations.

And in fact, even Mexico's rather mild interventions into the Texas economy were a chief cause of grumbling among the Anglo colonists, and the colonists' prodigious penchant for complaint caused Terán much concern. The government in Mexico City, the colonists charged, was lax about helping the colonists to expand their commercial prospects. The colonists had big dreams of a thriving agricultural export economy centered on cotton. Stephen F. Austin seldom tired of pointing out to Mexican officials that in only three decades the southern region of the United States had gone from exporting almost no cotton to exporting some six-hundred thousand bales. Texans were especially enthusiastic after 1828, when the United States passed the so-called "Tariff of Abominations," imposing high duties against imports of European manufactured goods, which in turn invited Europeans to retaliate against U.S. cotton growers by seeking alternative sources of supply. The Texans assumed this could work to their advantage if only the Mexican government would do its part by continuing indefinitely to waive tariffs on imports of machinery and other products essential for the cotton industry, and by authorizing new ports. They also hoped for stimulation of the coastal trade to provide commercial links between Texas and the rest of Mexico—something most Mexican statesmen favored also—but in fact little was done, and the coastal trade languished.

Texas's status as an appendage of the neighboring state of Coahuila was another cause for discontent among the colonists. At the time of the framing of the 1824 Constitution, Texas was deemed too poor and sparsely populated to merit statehood in its own right. Influential Texans favored creating Texas as a territory, meaning it would be administered directly by the central government, which presumably would provide development aid and protection from hostile Indians. An influential deputy from Coahuila, Miguel Ramos Arizpe, had maneuvered to link Texas to Coahuila, albeit with the provision that Texans could form their own state as soon as they felt able to do so. The link to Coahuila was unpopular with the Texans for several reasons. Coahuila, like Texas, was a poor state and was hence unable to provide much assistance. The newly created state, which carried the ungainly name Coahuila and Texas, had as its capital the dusty desert town of Saltillo, some seven hundred miles from the area of Anglo settlement in East Texas. The state's court of final appeals was located at Saltillo, and few lawyers in Texas were qualified to present cases before that court. This meant frequent arduous trips back and forth from the capital to visit a court that had little knowledge of, or sympathy for, the condition of the Texas settlers. In addition, Mexican law made no provision for trial by jury, something the colonists considered essential

to the well-being of the state. The Texans took to forming ju-
ries to try criminal cases on their own, even handing down
death sentences in defiance of Mexican law. Moreover, Texas
was clearly the subordinate partner in this arrangement, and
the Texans complained that the Coahuilans did not understand the needs of Texas in matters of economic development
and defense.

No issue was more vexing to the Texas colonists than slavery. The colonists were convinced that they could not possibly create a thriving agricultural economy without the use of
slaves. That, of course, placed them very much at odds with
the government in Mexico City and, indeed, with the rest of
the Mexican states. Slavery was practically nonexistent in
Mexico at the time of its independence, and the founders of
the republic regarded it with repugnance. A law was passed
on July 13, 1824, prohibiting "commerce and traffic in
slaves," but both the Constitution of 1824 and the federal colonization law of 1825 were silent on the issue and the July 13
law was subject to interpretation. Although the law did stipu-
late that slaves were to be considered free the instant they
trod Mexican soil, the Texas colonists elected to assume that
this referred only to the buying and selling of slaves and did
not apply to slaves brought by colonists for their own use.

The Texas colonists became adept at arguing that they be
made an exception to any law restricting slavery in the country. Proposed laws on the subject invariably brought an-
guished howls of protest from them, depicting widows and
orphans beggared, the land of Texas reverting to a howling
wilderness infested by savages and reprobates, and hardworking families brought to ruin. The colonists were remarkably
successful in their protests. In 1825 the committee writing a
constitution for the state of Coahuila and Texas considered a
provision that would have prohibited slavery "absolutely and
forever in all its territory, and slaves now in it shall be free
from the day the constitution is published in this capital." Af-

ter intense lobbying by the Anglo-Texans, the clause was watered down to provide only that children of slaves would be born free and that the migration of slaves into the state would be outlawed after six months. The colonists dealt with this provision by erecting the fiction that slaves were in fact indentured servants who had voluntarily contracted themselves to some years of labor.

The simple fact that Mexico officially disapproved of slavery and sought to protect the rights of slaves was, to the slave-owning colonists, a constant threat. According to Terán, it made the slaves restive and eager to "throw off their yoke, while their masters believe they can keep them by making [the yoke] heavier. They commit the barbarities on their slaves that are so common where men live in a relationship so contradictory to their nature: they pull their teeth, they set dogs upon them to tear them apart, and the mildest of them will whip the slaves until they are flayed."[5]

In the end General Terán and his colleagues came away with mixed impressions of the Texas colonists, their grudging admiration only adding to their apprehension. No doubt this bemusement contributed to the decidedly pessimistic mood of the commissioners as they completed their inspection. Their pessimism was also caused in part by the extreme hardships of the voyage. As the summer wore on, the commissioners ran short of food and were plagued by intolerable heat and dense clouds of noxious mosquitoes. Upon arriving at the Trinidad River, they decided to split up; three of the commission's members returned to San Antonio while Terán and Sánchez pushed on toward Nacogdoches. By that time, Sánchez reported, General Terán was "so melancholic that it made me fear for his valuable life."[6] He was also gravely ill, with gaunt, disfigured features and barely the strength to sit upright on his horse.

In their letters and reports, the commission members urged the Mexican government to take strong action to avoid losing Texas, but at the same time they appeared to regard that loss as practically a foregone conclusion. General Terán, while impressed by Austin and his colony, was convinced that inviting such colonization in the first place had been "folly" and that Mexico would have been better off had it simply allowed its northern regions to languish. "If it is bad for a nation to have vacant lands and wilderness," he wrote, "it is worse without a doubt to have settlers who cannot abide by some of its laws and the restrictions that [the nation] must place on commerce. They soon become discontent and thus prone to rebellion." The United States, he believed, would be quick to take advantage of such rebelliousness. "The North Americans have conquered whatever territory adjoins them . . . There is no power like that to the north, which by silent means has made conquests of momentous importance. Such dexterity, such constancy in their designs, such uniformity of means of execution which always are completely successful, arouses admiration."[7] Terán was prescient in his analysis of how the North Americans would proceed. They would, he wrote, eschew "armies, battles, or invasions, which make a great noise and for the most part are unsuccessful." They would instead follow a predictable if devious pattern, beginning by making extravagant and false statements purporting to demonstrate that they had a legitimate claim to Texas, then exciting public opinion in order to spur adventurers to take up residence in that state. Those new settlers would become more and more querulous, "discrediting the efficiency of the existing authority and administration; and the matter having arrived at this stage—which is precisely that of Texas at this moment—diplomatic maneuvers begin."[8]

Dramatic measures must be taken at once, Terán argued, or Texas would be lost. The measures he recommended were all eminently sensible. The military presence in Texas, he said, should be greatly increased; Mexicans should be given incentives to emigrate to Texas; other Europeans—preferably

Roman Catholics from Ireland, Switzerland, and Germany—should be invited to settle in Texas; and the coastal trade should be invigorated so as to increase the economic ties between Texas and the other states of the Mexican Republic. General Terán had a keen understanding of the essential problems: not only had Anglo-Americans come to greatly outnumber all other colonists in Texas, but they practiced a culture quite different from that of Mexico, and they owed their prosperity to trade with the United States. Outwitting such a dexterous and determined foe as the United States would surely be difficult, but Terán was in no mood to give up. There should be "a conviction in every Mexican heart," wrote the general, "that he who consents to or does not oppose the loss of Texas is an execrable traitor who ought to be punished with every kind of death."[9]

José María Sánchez, outdoing Terán in his pessimism, predicted that Mexico would in fact do nothing to thwart U.S. designs on Texas, either because it was perpetually involved "in those fatal convulsions that have destroyed the republic" or because Mexican authorities put faith in the reports of self-serving agents who continually assured them that Texas was under control. "Thus the vigilance of the highest authorities has been dulled while our enemies from the North do not lose a single opportunity of advancing though it be but a step towards their treacherous design which is well known."[10]

FATAL CONVULSIONS

Sánchez could not be accused of overstating the case when he bemoaned the "fatal convulsions" of Mexican politics. While the Boundary Commission was in Texas, the authorities in central Mexico were behaving as though intent on bearing out his point. In fact, during the Boundary Commission's brief existence, Mexico had three distinct governments. The commission was established by the government of Guadalupe

Victoria; it carried out its mission under the liberal regime of Vicente Guerrero; and it submitted its findings to yet a third government, the highly conservative and centralist regime of Anastasio Bustamante.

From the time he had assumed the presidency in early 1829, Vicente Guerrero, a man of mixed race and a hero to poor Mexicans, found himself under increasing pressure from conservatives who regarded him as illegitimate because of his ethnicity and because he had seized power after losing the presidential election. But he managed to alienate them through his policies as well. Guerrero, heavily influenced by his finance minister, the radical federalist Lorenzo de Zavala, pushed through a number of measures intended to appeal to liberals and the poor. His government promulgated a second law expelling Spaniards from the country, this one more draconian than the first. Guerrero's administration also reformed the tax system, shifting the heaviest burden of taxation onto medium and large businesses, foreigners, and the rich, leading predictably to howls of protest from conservatives. Tariff policy, too, proved contentious. From the late colonial period onward Mexico had embraced the principles of free trade, allowing cheap, high-quality textiles to flood into the Mexican market. Urban artisans, cotton farmers, and would-be textile manufacturers depended on the domestic textile industry, but they could offer only anemic competition to British industries, which moved aggressively to capture Latin American markets for their industrial products. Consumers eagerly snapped up *sarapes* manufactured in the mills of Glasgow in preference to inferior and more costly local products, and the chorus of complaints from those displaced by imports rose steadily. Guerrero placed high tariffs on imported textiles, which pleased artisans but made him enemies among consumers, importers, and foreign businessmen.

Adding to the tumult, the Spanish government chose this moment to attempt a reconquest of Mexico, which it continued obstinately to consider the jewel in the crown of its empire. Angered by the expulsion laws, and wildly overoptimistic about the prospects for a successful invasion, the Spaniards imagined they could defeat the Mexicans with an expeditionary force of only twenty-eight hundred soldiers. That force came ashore on a beach near the port of Tampico in late July 1829. The Spaniards, apparently assuming the Mexican government was so unpopular that the Mexican people would rally to their cause, did not bother to bring horses or artillery, for these items were to be commandeered from sympathetic Mexicans. Nature treated the Spaniards harshly, as yellow fever took an alarming toll on the Spanish troops and a hurricane rocked the Gulf Coast just in time for the climactic engagement. Under the leadership of Generals Antonio López de Santa Anna and Manuel de Mier y Terán, recently returned from his expedition to Texas, the Mexicans prevailed. The Spanish invasion force surrendered ignominiously on September 11 after a charge by a Mexican army of only around nine hundred men.

The defeat of the Spanish expeditionary force was the first good news the Mexicans had heard in years, and they took it as an occasion for exuberant patriotic revelry, full of church bells, orchestras, speeches, fireworks, and plenty of liquor. The matter might have seemed trivial had it taken place during more tranquil times, but in the overheated environment of 1829 it turned out to have enormous consequences. Both Santa Anna and Terán were named Beneméritos de la Patria, the highest honor the Mexican government could bestow. Terán's newly elevated status would make his warnings regarding Texas hard to dismiss. Santa Anna, for his part, solidified his reputation as Mexico's greatest soldier. Distinguished citizens tussled for the honor of carrying the great man on their shoulders; a medal was struck in his honor with the inscription "At Tampico he struck down Spanish arrogance." September 11 was declared a national holiday, and it was celebrated as long as Santa Anna wielded influence in Mexico. The Spanish invasion, then, provided Mexico with a hero and a savior in whom many Mexicans felt they could invest their most sincere and complete faith. Santa Anna would spend the next decades abusing that faith.

The patriotic fervor did not last long. President Guerrero had been under attack before the invasion, and he gained a very brief respite from it. But soon the attacks were renewed with still greater vehemence, for now was added the charge that Guerrero was refusing to relinquish the emergency powers he had been granted to deal with the Spanish invasion and that he was shamelessly abusing those powers. He had seized the opportunity to issue an emergency decree outlawing slavery throughout the Mexican Republic, a clear slap at the Texans (even though the Texans requested and were granted an exemption from the decree). He also decreed punishment for any publication subverting independence and federalism, and Finance Minister Zavala decreed special taxes to help Mexico confront the emergency. Guerrero scored a few points with conservatives by finally expelling U.S. ambassador Joel Poinsett from the country. But an armed rebellion nevertheless erupted, and the very same day Poinsett departed—Christmas Day, 1829—Guerrero was himself forced to surrender the presidency.

Conservatives, who by now were openly styling themselves hombres de bien, were determined that their regime should restore law, order, and morality to Mexico. All around them they saw chaos and decay. The Roman Catholic Church—for conservative Mexicans, the proudest pillar of the old colonial regime—was a pale shadow of its former glory, its priesthood decimated, its cathedrals untended, and its wealth diminished. More alarming still, the army was in a lamentable state. The trend toward rebellion and counterrebellion that had become manifest in the late 1820s meant that the army was heavily politicized and top-heavy with generals who owed their rank

to having backed a winning side, not to any special competence in military matters. Some officers in the provinces built
up their own bases of support, becoming veritable warlords
who were well beyond the central government's control. The
continuing political turmoil gave these men ample room to
maneuver.

Recruiting for the army was another perennial problem.
For a time officials had tried recruiting by lottery, but news
of recruiting parties was hard to keep secret: able-bodied
men would flee their villages well in advance of the recruiters'
arrival. Some states decreed that all vagrants, criminals, bach-
elors, and widowers without children must serve. Unscrupulous recruiters used deception or force to fill their quotas, at
times carrying their recruits away in chains. The army's rank
and file came to consist largely of impoverished Indians,
hardened criminals, and the wretched poor of the cities. Soldiers' wages commonly went unpaid, and money was often
lacking for even the most basic necessities. Officers were
sometimes forced to use their personal credit to obtain supplies or to commandeer funds from customs houses or com-
missaries. Even when supplies were available, soldiers would
sometimes sell them for ready cash, creating a thriving black
market in military equipment. Not surprisingly, desertion was
a chronic problem, and discipline was very poor indeed. Officers were chagrined to confess that, during the Spanish
invasion, homes at Tampico were looted not by the enemy
soldiers but by Mexican soldiers.

Compounding the problems of the military was the existence of so-called civic militias, which had been created for
local defense but which, by the late 1820s, had become bas-
tions of local sovereignty, the shock troops of state governors
in their ongoing disputes with the center. The civic militia of
Zacatecas, whose governor Francisco García was perhaps the
era's most assertive federalist, boasted more than seventeen
thousand men; that of Yucatán a comparable number. To con-

servatives, the civic militias were emblematic of the general decline of Mexican society, more armed mobs than disciplined fighting forces, and they presented most unwelcome competition for the national army. They increased the uncomfortable sense that Mexico was literally pulling itself apart, its chances of achieving genuine nationhood growing ever more remote.

Adding further to this bleak picture, the financial woes of the central government were dire. In the early days after independence, Mexico had contracted a pair of loans with British commercial houses that forced it to pledge two-thirds of its customs revenues to repayment. The loans, moreover, were made on harsh terms, such that Mexico was obliged to repay some 32 million pesos in exchange for just over seventeen thousand. Revenues the government hoped to collect from taxing the export of silver and cochineal, a valuable dyestuff made from dried insects, failed to materialize as Mexico's productivity declined precipitously. Revenue-sharing plans worked out with the states led to chronic disputes in which the central government's treasury usually came up the loser. By 1827 Mexico had to default on the repayment of the British loans and thus forfeited any hope of receiving additional international loans. In order merely to meet basic operating expenses, the government was reduced to borrowing money at usurious rates of interest from unscrupulous private moneylenders known as *agiotistas*. And so the debt mounted.

Added to all of this was still more tangible evidence of decay. The port of Veracruz, Mexico's economic lifeline, had been repeatedly bombarded by the Spaniards in the years after independence. By the mid-1820s it was a virtual ghost town, with empty homes, weed-choked streets, and vast hordes of black turkey buzzards lurking on rooftops and in tree branches. Mexico City, once the elegant capital of the Viceroyalty of New Spain, also presented a rancid spectacle. According to an official publication, the capital city's "streets are no longer worthy of the name; they are chasms, precipices and filthy sewers. Its suburbs are heaps of ruins, horrific dungheaps, centers of corruption and pestilence. Its avenues are now no more than remnants of what they once were. Its most public thoroughfares are places of scandal and indecency and there is a tavern, vice and prostitution on almost every street. Nowhere is safe from crime."[11] Small wonder, then, that the hombres de bien found themselves afflicted with an incurable and worsening nostalgia for colonial times, for the days before Mexicans had offended God with their newfangled liberal ideas. But turning back the clock would not be easy.

Guerrero was replaced in the presidency by Anastasio Bustamante, a former royalist army officer with a legendary fondness for women and soft-boiled eggs. Bustamante was reputed to be an honest and decent man, but he was also notoriously indecisive, slow-witted, and lacking in strong political conviction. The real power in the Bustamante administration was exercised by his secretary of interior and exterior affairs, Lucas Alamán, who was indisputably brilliant but had a decidedly authoritarian bent and a rather vindictive nature. The Bustamante government launched an all-out assault against its political opponents, the federalists. The stated aim of the government's policy was to remove all public officials "against whom public opinion has been expressed"—a conveniently vague and sweeping category. Alamán engineered a thoroughgoing purge of federalist governors and legislators in the states. In the national congress, opposition deputies were arrested and deposed, many of them savagely beaten and intimidated. In March 1830 some two hundred people were arrested in Mexico City on charges of conspiracy. Opposition periodicals were shut down, their headquarters raided, and their presses destroyed. Many prominent federalists went underground or fled the country. The government also endeavored to suppress the civic militias by placing them under the

direct control of the regular army. Some of the old heroes of
the independence wars found themselves denounced. Vicente
Guerrero, the most prominent of the lot, was labeled "mentally and morally unfit for office." This was, in the words of a
government paper, nothing less than "a war of civilization
against barbarism, of property against thieves, of order
against anarchy."[12] Dissent had become dangerous.

THE LAW OF APRIL 6, 1830

It fell to the Bustamante government to receive the report of
Terán's Boundary Commission, with its detailed insistence
that immediate steps must be taken if Mexico hoped to retain
Texas. The regime faced up boldly to the challenge by passing
the so-called Law of April 6, 1830. The April 6 Law adopted
virtually all of Terán's recommendations. It used revenues
from duties on imports of cotton textiles to provide funding
for the military effort "to maintain the integrity of Mexican
territory." According to the law, commissioners would be sent
from Mexico to secure lands for colonies of Mexicans in the
northern frontier states, and those commissioners were to see
that those lands were peopled. Convict soldiers, instead of being confined in dank dungeons, would be sent northward,
where they would be put to work building fortifications, public works, and roads. Mexican families who expressed a desire
to become colonists would be provided free transportation
and the best available farmland. Foreigners hoping to enter
Texas would have to show valid Mexican passports. Coastal
trade would be free from customs duties for four years, with
the object of developing regular trading contacts between
Mexico's northern states and the Gulf Coast ports of Matamoros, Tampico, and Veracruz. The most controversial provisions of the law were aimed squarely and unsubtly at the
Anglo-American settlers. They declared that the federal
authorities would strictly enforce the prohibition on the im-

portation of slaves into Mexican territory, and no more Americans would be permitted to settle in Texas. All empresario contracts not already completed were suspended.

The Anglo-Americans of Texas were, not surprisingly, outraged by the law, even though in fact it had no immediate impact. The prohibition on further importation of slaves was moot. The state of Coahuila and Texas already had such a law, and the Texans had been successfully evading it for some time with the ruse of pretending their slaves were indentured servants working under contract for the colonists. The prohibition on further immigration from the United States would clearly be meaningless, too, so long as Mexico lacked the means to enforce it. General Terán was profoundly aware of these facts. The Guerrero government had appointed him commandant general for the Eastern Interior Provinces, as the states of Tamaulipas and Coahuila and Texas were known. That meant that he was charged with making the law's provisions a reality, a task he apparently assumed would be impossible. He was, however, determined to give it a valiant effort.

The obstacles were daunting. According to the plan, state governors were to be instrumental in aiding the scheme to settle Mexicans in Texas. But state governors were fiercely jealous of their sovereignty. General Terán already had some experience with how recalcitrant they could be. Back in 1829 he had planned a military expedition to Texas, hoping to impress the fractious foreign colonists with a show of Mexican resolve. The minister of war instructed the governors of Guadalajara, Guanajuato, Zacatecas, and Durango to send contingents of soldiers to the northern town of Matamoros, where they were to place themselves under Terán's orders. The governors were deliberately slow in complying with the order, and Zacatecas governor Francisco García flatly refused on the grounds that the federal government had no constitutional right to order troops from one state to serve in another. The Law of April 6 did nothing to remedy this fundamental problem. General Terán began his colonization effort by sending letters to state governors instructing them to gather families for relocation to Texas, where they would be granted lands and financial assistance for one year. Most of the governors simply ignored his first two requests. The third they answered with the curt assertion that it was unfair to ask them to furnish people from their states in order to strengthen another state. As it turned out, only one Mexican family was actually sent to Texas under the plan. Only one individual, a schoolteacher from Tula, requested government assistance in relocating there. Ironically, this lone request was denied on the grounds that no families were going to Texas, so there would be no need for schoolteachers.

The plan to send convict soldiers to man the Texas garrisons also met with resistance, and by early 1831 Terán was forced to accept the reality that Mexicans simply could not be persuaded to head north. He did not abandon the effort to counterbalance Anglo-American influence, however. He desperately explored other avenues, such as persuading the Cherokee Indians to accept Catholicism, the Spanish language, and Mexican law and become settled farmers. This effort was undercut by Cherokee skepticism, meager numbers, and Terán's own prejudices, for he seems to have feared that the Indians could not be fully civilized and might end up more of a problem than the Anglo-Americans. Terán was also cool to a proposal to form a colony of fifty thousand free blacks from Cuba, and that project too failed to materialize. Mexican diplomats in European cities placed ads in newspapers promoting the wonders of Texas and inviting immigrants, but the Europeans did not take the bait, and so Anglo-Americans continued to dominate the population of Texas. Terán had to content himself with establishing new forts at strategic points and giving those forts names intended to inspire patriotism with their primordial Mexicanness: Tenochtitlán on the Brazos River, Anáhuac at Galveston Bay, Lipantitlán on the Nueces.

For Terán, the fundamental problem in retaining Texas was economic. Since 1800 the United States had undergone rapid and sweeping economic transformations. During the early decades of the nineteenth century the Americans had feverishly built roads, bridges, canals, telegraph lines, railways, and steam engines. By the 1820s the country was beginning a period of frantic urbanization, and mechanized industries were thriving. While Mexico slid deeper into poverty and despair, the United States was giddily optimistic, a "scene of unmingled prosperity and happiness," in the words of a Fourth of July speaker of the 1830s.[13] The United States had emerged as a modern capitalist nation, and the spirit of nationalism in the country was strong and growing. It is hardly surprising that the Anglo-Americans who settled in Texas should wish to partake of U.S. prosperity. Their chief economic ties were to U.S. rather than to Mexican ports, and those ties served them well. General Terán gave serious thought to placing legal impediments to the Texas-U.S. trade, but he soon realized that doing this would surely provoke a confrontation with the settlers that he could not hope to stifle with the paltry numbers of soldiers at his disposal.

That much became clear in the fateful years of 1831 and 1832. Much of the friction of those years involved tariffs. Part of the inducement that Mexico had used early on to attract settlers to Texas was exemption from tariff duties for a period of seven years. Colonists had become accustomed to the duty-free importation of all manner of tools and supplies, mostly from the United States, and they resented it when Mexican authorities began imposing tariffs and new regulations in 1830. Adding to the colonists' ire, customs collector George Fisher issued an order requiring all ships putting in at Texas ports to register at Anáhuac. That meant that captains

of ships putting in at Brazoria, at the mouth of the Brazos
River, had to make an arduous hundred-mile overland trek
to clear their papers. The order was the occasion for an exchange of heated letters between Stephen F. Austin and General Terán, with Austin contending that the settlers "have just
causes and very many to complain," and Terán angrily reply-
ing that every nation in the world collected customs duties at
their ports, but "only at Brazoria [are] they considered cause
for violence."[14] Terán soon cooled down and granted that the
settlers' complaints had merit. A branch of the customs house
was installed at Brazoria to collect taxes on the Brazos River
traffic. Even so American ships routinely disregarded the customs houses altogether, and the undermanned Mexican garrisons found they could do little about it. In December 1831
three ships passed the Anáhuac fort without paying their duties, leading to an exchange of gunfire in which a Mexican
soldier was wounded.

Anglo-American colonists in Texas also complained bitterly about the federal commander of the Anáhuac garrison at
Galveston Bay, a Kentuckian named Juan Davis Bradburn, by
all accounts an extremely arrogant individual. The colonists
charged that Bradburn was overzealous in enforcing unpopular Mexican laws. He interfered when Coahuila and Texas authorities granted land titles in East Texas to Anglo-Americans
in violation of the Law of April 6; and he provided refuge
to a pair of runaway slaves from Louisiana who found their
way to his post, following up this action by arresting the slave
owner's lawyer. In June 1832 Anglo settlers headed to
Anáhuac intending to mount an assault. The garrison at the
Velasco fort, at the mouth of the Brazos, tried to impede
them, and after a firefight in which perhaps twelve men were
killed and thirty wounded, the Mexican garrison surrendered.
Further fighting at Anáhuac was averted only by the judicious
intervention of Colonel José de las Piedras of the Nacogdoches garrison, who rushed to reinforce Bradburn but man-

aged skillfully to placate the angry settlers. It was shortly after these episodes that the tax collectors and soldiers recognized the futility of their task. They were also needed elsewhere, as a fresh revolution was just then heating up in central Mexico. They simply abandoned their posts.

The difficulties in central Mexico were shaping up to be the most serious Mexico had yet endured. The deposed president Vicente Guerrero, along with fellow southern caudillo Juan Alvarez, had risen up in arms against the Bustamante government in March 1830. Their rebellion appeared to portend the conservative elite's worst nightmare: Guerrero, speaking his Indian language, harangued his troops to avenge themselves against the whites, thus conjuring the fearsome specter of race war. Guerrero fell prisoner in January 1831, and in February the swarthy hero of independence was court-martialed and executed. It was an unusually savage sentence, for it was far more customary to send rebels into exile, sometimes even furnishing them with a comfortable government pension. Many surmised that Guerrero's execution was an act of racial vindictiveness, and it caused widespread revulsion, permanently tarnishing the reputations of Bustamante's cabinet officers.

In January 1832, egged on by a committee of embattled dissidents based in Mexico City, General Santa Anna launched a rebellion against the Bustamante government from Veracruz. By summer that rebellion had blossomed into a full-fledged civil war, and Bustamante was ousted by the end of the year.

General Terán kept abreast of all these developments from his headquarters in the tiny pueblo of Padilla, Tamaulipas. On the afternoon of July 2, 1832, he wrote to his friend Lucas Alamán in Mexico City, expressing his unrelieved despair. Mexico would never emerge, he wrote, from the disasters that had overtaken it, and soon the constant infighting of ambitious and selfish men would cost Mexico its northern provinces. How could Mexico possibly keep Texas, he wondered, if Mexicans could not agree among themselves? What, he asked again and again, would become of Texas? The beauty and brilliance of the natural world, he lamented, contrasted depressingly with the tiny village of Padilla, a squalid ruin surrounded by ashen adobe walls. "I am an unhappy man," he wrote, "and unhappy people should not live on earth."

The next morning he rose early and donned his full dress uniform, complete with medals and insignia and a brightly colored silk handkerchief at the collar. He made a short tour of the dusty plaza, then walked to the ruined shell of the church of San Antonio de Padilla. There he fixed his sword's handle against the wall, placed the blade to his heart, lurched forward, and ended his life.

4

SANTA ANNA AND THE
TEXAS REVOLUTION

The two years following Terán's suicide confirmed the general's darkest forebodings. Mexico's own political troubles continued unabated, while the Texas colonists grew steadily more restive. Both federalists and centralists had a chance to solve the Texas problem, but Mexico found itself unable to create a credible counterweight to the Anglo-Americans of Texas; nor could it placate them. Texas, just as General Terán had predicted, continued to slip inexorably away.

SANTA ANNA TAKES CHARGE

The 1830–32 government of Anastasio Bustamante, steered mostly by Bustamante's chief adviser Lucas Alamán, could claim some modest achievements. It had established a government bank using funds from protectionist tariffs; that, in turn, enabled the regime to set up Mexico's first cotton mills, which enjoyed a modest boom in the ensuing years. Bustamante's government managed even to somewhat improve

Mexico's malignant image among foreign investors and lenders and to establish peace with the Vatican. But the regime's vindictiveness—seen most glaringly in the execution of Vicente Guerrero, a bona fide national hero—earned it much enmity; and there was always plenty of ready-made enmity among those who had inflexible ideological objections to a centralist regime.

In January 1832 Santa Anna rose in arms against the Bustamante government. At that moment he was well positioned to benefit both from the popular outrage at the Guerrero execution—Santa Anna was consistent in few things, but his support for Guerrero had been unswerving—and from the popular acclaim he had gained for his part in defeating the Spanish invasion of 1829. Santa Anna's main partner in expelling the Spaniards, General Manuel de Mier y Terán, remained loyal to Bustamante. Terán was widely seen as the only man in Mexico who had the prestige and popularity to bridge the vast chasm between the factions: twelve of nineteen legislatures polled in 1832 favored him for the presidency. Terán's suicide left the stage open to Santa Anna. It was an unfortunate final act, for Santa Anna's key talent lay in exploiting political divisions, not in healing them. The Texas colonists, for their part, seized upon General Terán's exit to abandon caution, openly embracing Santa Anna's cause in the hope that his triumph would mean greater autonomy for the states.

The Texans complained of excessive taxes, unfair tariff policies, and aristocratic despotism. They hoped that Santa Anna's triumph would mean curtailment of the power of the church and army, separation of Texas from Coahuila, abrogation of the Law of April 6, 1830, and economic privileges—the whole package of reforms for which they had long agitated. But many who embraced what they took to be Santa Anna's cause had reason to distrust the man himself. Austin

referred to him as a "sort of Mad Cap difficult to class."[1]
Despite a host of misgivings, when elections were held in
March 1833, Santa Anna was the resounding victor.

Although Santa Anna was a veteran of political intrigue,
this was his first stint as president. He would go on to serve
as president of the republic on ten more occasions, and he
wielded considerable power even when he did not occupy the
presidency. He was undoubtedly the most important Mexican
political figure of his day. His tremendous influence and
longevity have long presented historians with a conundrum.
Santa Anna's flaws were numerous and widely acknowledged,
even during his own time. Mexicans ever since have blamed
him for many, if not most, of the misfortunes their country
suffered during the middle decades of the nineteenth century.
He gave his contemporaries every conceivable cause to mistrust him, for he betrayed every constituency that ever rallied
on his behalf. It is therefore somewhat difficult to explain why
the Mexicans—including men of clear integrity and intelli-
gence—solicited his services again and again, convinced that
he represented the country's best, and perhaps only, hope.

There are several explanations for Santa Anna's enduring
appeal, none of them entirely satisfying. In fact, although
he was vain, corrupt, incompetent, and untrustworthy, Santa
Anna boasted a number of qualities that helped to make him
the indispensable man of his generation. Specifically, he was
cruel, addicted to risk, rich, geographically well situated, ideo-
logically mutable, and charismatic.

Santa Anna gained his earliest military experience fighting
for the Spanish army against hostile Indians and rebellious
settlers during the independence wars. It was presumably
here that he was schooled in the give-no-quarter, take-no-
prisoners methods of the Spanish army, and he developed a
penchant for cruelty. To some, a willingness to use harsh
methods looked much like decisiveness, an unsentimental de-

termination to get the job done regardless of the cost in blood and treasure. At many times those qualities seemed precisely what Mexico needed.

Santa Anna was also an incorrigible gambler. He seldom let his political or military duties interfere with his enjoyment of his beloved cockfights. He attended cockfighting conventions that went on for up to a week, and winning or losing six thousand pesos a day was nothing unusual. He was willing to gamble with Mexico's fortunes, too, and the risks he took sometimes paid off handsomely. While others deliberated, Santa Anna took action, his recklessness often appearing as selfless patriotism. For example, when the Spaniards invaded in 1829, it took him less than a week to gather a force of sixteen hundred men; he then commandeered merchant ships to move his impromptu infantry up the coast while another contingent marched overland; and he hastily secured the funds to buy supplies and munitions. His reputation for boldness in crisis situations, then, was not undeserved. And his formidable gift for self-promotion ensured that his heroism would not be forgotten.

Santa Anna was quite wealthy, his wealth being both a source and a perquisite of power. He greatly enhanced his fortune in 1825 when, at the age of thirty-one, he married the fourteen-year-old daughter of a wealthy Spanish merchant who brought with her a substantial dowry in money and land. He eventually came to own nearly half a million acres in the state of Veracruz. His haciendas (as large rural estates were called) were profitable working farms and ranches with hundreds of employees and thousands of head of livestock. Income from these properties, supplemented by the generous salaries he was paid as a public servant and by illicit income from all manner of shady dealings, meant that Santa Anna was, in modern terms, a millionaire several times over.

The haciendas, and especially Santa Anna's favorite, Manga de Clavo, were more than a source of material riches.

They assured Santa Anna of a solid regional power base. Santa Anna closely fit the mold of the caudillo, a common enough character in nineteenth-century Latin America. Caudillos were men who managed to build regional power through deft combinations of kinship, charisma, patronage, shrewd understanding of the common folk, and control of strategic resources. In accordance with this pattern, Santa Anna was able to pack the civilian and military bureaucracies of Veracruz with cronies and kinsmen and to put together whole armies out of local supporters and employees. Santa Anna's passion for gambling brought him into daily contact with a cross-section of Mexican society, from highborn officers to peasants, thieves, and rascals, affording him a keen understanding of his nation's culture and mores. Santa Anna owned haciendas in both the sweltering lowlands around the city of Veracruz and in the cooler tropical highlands near Jalapa, straddling the country's most valuable trading route and most important strategic corridor. Those who rebelled against the Mexico City government during the nineteenth century routinely sought to control Veracruz so they could commandeer customs revenues. The Veracruz-Jalapa route had been standard for foreign invaders of Mexico since the days of Cortés, so Santa Anna's knowledge of that part of the country gave him a tremendous home-field advantage during those tumultuous times. And his regional base also gave him immunity to the dreaded tropical diseases of the coast that wreaked such havoc among foreigners and highlanders. Santa Anna, then, provides perhaps the ultimate proof that nineteenth-century Mexico was less than the sum of its parts, and that whoever controlled the critical parts controlled, to a perilous degree, the nation's destiny.

In a time when ideological inflexibility was a crippling affliction in Mexico, Santa Anna's lack of convictions was a positive asset. His one reasonably secure conviction, in fact, was a disdain for the popular will, which freed him to act with little fear of political consequences. According to his own account, Santa Anna had advocated democracy early in his career but had soon seen the folly of it. "A hundred years to come," he once told U.S. ambassador Joel Poinsett, "my people will not be fit for liberty. They do not know what it is, unenlightened as they are, and under the influence of a Catholic clergy, a despotism is the proper government for them, but there is no reason why it should not be a wise and virtuous one."[2] Politics, for Santa Anna, seems to have been primarily the art of finding the perfect despot, and for him that search usually ended satisfactorily only with himself.

Finally Santa Anna, for all his faults, was by nearly all accounts a uniquely charismatic man, nothing at all like the vain and buffoonish figure who gallops so recklessly through the history books. In fact, those who met him were mostly struck by the sobriety and gravity of his character. Brantz Mayer, an American diplomat who was cynical about Mexican politics generally and about Santa Anna specifically, could not help being impressed. Santa Anna's expression, Mayer reported, "is that of mingled pain and anxiety. In perfect repose, you would think him looking on a dying friend, with whose sufferings he was deeply but helplessly sympathizing . . . you feel that you have before you a man, who would be singled from a thousand for his quiet refinement and serious temper; one who would at once command your sympathy and your respect."[3] Another foreigner, Fanny Calderón de la Barca, had a remarkably similar impression: "Knowing nothing of his past history, one would have said a philosopher, living in dignified retirement—one who had tried the world, and found that all was vanity—one who had suffered ingratitude, and who, if he were ever persuaded to emerge from his retreat, would only do so, Cincinnatus-like, to benefit his country. It is strange, how frequently this expression of philosophic resignation, of placid sadness, is to be remarked on the countenances of the deepest, most ambitious, and most designing men."[4]

Mrs. Calderón—who did indeed know something of Santa Anna's history—was astute in her suspicion that Santa Anna's demeanor was a carefully crafted pose designed to keep his interlocutors off guard. The attitude of world-weariness she observed was also useful: Santa Anna would surely have been flattered by the analogy to Cincinnatus, the humble farmer of Roman legend who sallied forth to save his people from an encroaching enemy, then eschewed all honors and titles on the grounds that he was merely a selfless servant of the Roman Republic. In hopes of conveying precisely that message, Santa Anna, upon attaining power, would invariably relinquish that power at once, retiring to his hacienda and insisting that he wished only to return to a tranquil private life. There, according to his own account, he would sleep a lot and drink enormous quantities of milk, waiting more or less patiently for the situation to deteriorate to the point where his countrymen would implore his heroic intervention. In the Mexico of the early nineteenth century, it was a fairly safe bet that the situation would deteriorate.

Such was the strategy Santa Anna adopted in March 1833, after his election to the presidency. After suppressing an abortive rebellion against his government, he asked congress for permission to take leave from the presidency so he could recover his health. That meant that during his absence his vice president, Valentín Gómez Farías, would be in charge.

Gómez Farías was renowned for his sincerity and honesty, but conservatives dreaded his outspoken liberalism. He was a physician and former professor who hailed from Guadalajara, Jalisco, a federalist stronghold. An enthusiast for French political theory, he believed strongly in individual freedom, universal male suffrage, social equality, and free trade—that is, the definitive destruction of what was left of the old colonial ethos. Santa Anna decided to give Gómez Farías space to enact the sort of liberal reforms he was bound to enact, then observe the response. If Gómez Farías proved more powerful and successful than his adversaries, Santa Anna could take credit for his achievements. If he went too far and alienated too many powerful people, Santa Anna would take the lead in ensuring his demise. Either way, Santa Anna would come out the winner.

Unlike many of his contemporaries, Gómez Farías felt that Mexico was, at least within certain limits, ready for a program of progressive reforms, and as predicted, he took the opportunity afforded him by Santa Anna's leave of absence to put such reforms into effect. Unfortunately, his government was no more subtle or compromising in liberalizing Mexico than the Bustamante regime had been in centralizing power. Just as the hombres de bien believed that Mexico's well-being depended on power remaining concentrated in their own hands, Gómez Farías believed with equal fervor that it depended on wresting power from those same entrenched privileged groups and distributing wealth and power more equitably among the general populace. A key step in the transformation Gómez Farías envisioned for the country was to remove conservative elites from all positions of authority. Hundreds, perhaps thousands, of civil servants at the federal and local levels were unceremoniously fired and replaced by liberals. In the army, senior officers who were thought to be opposed to liberal reforms—including General Anastasio Bustamante, till recently president of the republic—were dismissed or demoted, their pensions confiscated and their reputations impugned. Arrest orders went out for several cabinet members from the Bustamante administration on charges of complicity in the murder of General Vicente Guerrero. From Supreme Court justices to bishops, many prominent people were charged with a variety of offenses. The crowning act in this vindictive campaign was the so-called Ley del Caso of June 1833, which listed some fifty-one prominent persons and ordered them all summarily into exile. At the same time a renewed campaign for the expulsion of still more Spaniards began.

Radical propagandists advocated all-out class warfare in their effort to attract popular support. Liberal newspapers focused on the vast gulf between rich and poor, suggesting ways to narrow the gap: a progressive income tax, for example, or agrarian reform. Perhaps the most energetic of Gómez Farías's policies aimed to curtail the power of the Roman Catholic Church. The assault began with government orders that priests be prohibited from commenting on politics from the pulpit and that they be removed from the business of educating the young. Shortly thereafter came a decree suppressing Mexico's principal university on the grounds it was dominated by priests, and then another saying the government would no longer assume responsibility for tithe collection or the enforcement of monastic vows. The administration also gave notice to the church that the government, not the pope, would henceforth appoint top church officials, and it secularized the missions in California.

At the same time the government worked to reduce the size of the federal army and to deprive officers of their military *fuero*, or immunity from civil prosecution, while expanding and strengthening the local civic militias. Conservatives feared the worst: soon the clergy, too, would lose their fuero and their property, and attacks on the army and church would accelerate the country's headlong descent into barbarism. Conservatives scorned liberal congressmen as troglodytes who were merely putting on airs with their gloves and dress coats. They sought salvation in the person of the man who in fact was already president of the republic, Antonio López de Santa Anna.

Santa Anna, from his hacienda, had been quietly allowing Gómez Farías to believe that the liberal reform program had his blessings. In fact, however, Santa Anna had been entertaining complaints from many sectors. In April 1834 Santa Anna returned to the capital and made it clear that he had had a change of heart and now supported the conservatives and centralists. He issued a proclamation saying he did not support the liberal reforms, pressuring Gómez Farías into exile. In effect, Santa Anna overthrew his own government. He then invited back into positions of power the very people he had overthrown only a little more than a year previously and set about constructing what the hombres de bien had been wanting all along: a highly centralized, authoritarian regime.

THE TEXAS REVOLUTION

Santa Anna's sudden turn toward centralism was a key moment in paving the way for the U.S.-Mexican War, for the Texas colonists would insist that it gave them just cause to rebel.

In May 1835 Mexico's new centralist congress declared it had a mandate to write a new constitution. That constitution, known as the Seven Laws, instituted new property and literacy qualifications for citizenship and eligibility for public office; strengthened the office of president, extending his term to eight years; eliminated the office of vice president; and instituted a new and innovative branch of government known as the Supreme Conservative Power, with extremely broad powers, to mediate among the executive, legislative, and judicial branches. (This innovation was likely devised as a hedge against Santa Anna's authoritarian tendencies.) The document worsened class antagonisms by eliminating all hope of political influence for the poor. New property qualifications for voting and officeholding excluded not only the rural poor, who seldom participated in politics anyway, but also artisans, the unemployed, and domestic servants, who comprised perhaps 80 percent of the urban population. The new constitution also restricted political officeholding by age, with the minimum age for a town council post set at twenty-five years, and the minimum age for president at forty. Since life expectancy among the poor was about twenty-seven years, this helped further to restrict officeholding to the affluent, who naturally tended to live longer.

The new citizenship restrictions did not rankle the Texans nearly as much as the constitution's frank suppression of federalism. Ironically, the extreme centralization of power was inspired at least in part by Mexican fears of losing Texas. Centralists noted that the U.S. press was openly advocating the annexation of Texas. Suppressing states' rights, they argued, was essential to eliminate that threat. The Seven Laws did away with state legislatures and made state governors appointees of the central government. States were henceforth to be known as "departments," and they had virtually no autonomy. At the same time Santa Anna's government ordered a drastic reduction in the size of the state militias. Although the Seven Laws were not formally adopted until the end of 1836, it was quite clear by mid-1835 that Santa Anna's new government was no friend of the states.

The centralizing reforms of 1835 did not come as an epiphany to the Texans. In fact, the spirit of rebellion there had been building steadily for years. The series of flare-ups against tariff collection that began in late 1831 had tended to suggest that Stephen Austin's conciliatory posture was falling out of favor. During those earlier disturbances Austin had frankly criticized his rebellious fellow Texans: "I can assure the whole colony and all Texas that nothing but the outrageous imprudence of the people themselves will bring trouble on that country. If the whole of the settlers will adopt my motto, *Fidelity to Mexico*, and act and talk in conformity, they will flourish beyond their own expectations."[5] But Austin was nevertheless convinced that certain changes were necessary in the Texas-Mexico relationship, and despite his talk of fidelity he gave his blessings to several moderately rebellious moves. In 1832 the Texans seconded Santa Anna's federalist rebellion against the Bustamante government in the hope that it would lead to the reforms they favored. At the same time it was decided that a simple statement of adherence to the rebellion was not sufficient: the Texans must form a party to support their positions.

So in October 1832, while central Mexico was engulfed in civil war, Austin's colonists held a convention that resulted in a demand that the Mexican government repeal Article 11 of the Law of April 6, 1830—that is, the article banning further immigration of Americans into Texas. They also demanded exemption of certain goods from the tariff for ten years; the granting of land titles to certain settlers in East Texas, theretofore considered squatters; and the separation of Texas from Coahuila. Texas state officials declared the convention illegal, but the colonists held a second convention in April 1833 where they reaffirmed their earlier demands and adopted a provisional constitution for the state of Texas.

This second convention is notable partly because of the presence of some new members, most especially Sam Houston. Houston's colorful résumé included two years living with the Cherokee Indians, a stint in Congress, and an uncompleted term as governor of Tennessee. He was also a close friend of President Andrew Jackson, a man who had made no secret of his desire to acquire Texas. Houston represented a new spirit of radicalism in favor of outright independence for Texas. At the convention he aired his frank doubts as to whether the Texans would be able to continue living under Mexican rule. He chaired the committee that drafted the proposed state constitution for Texas, one that was copied almost verbatim from the Massachusetts constitution of 1780—an odd thing, considering the vast differences between Massachusetts in 1780 and a frontier state of the Mexican Republic in 1833. The intent may well have been to send a signal to the Mexicans that Texas was more American than Mexican.

If so, the signal was not lost on the authorities at San Antonio, who refused to support the Anglo-Texans in their efforts. The San Antonio authorities shared many of the same com-

plaints of the Anglo-Texans, but they were also far more pre-
occupied with simply securing their place within a Mexican
federal republic, and they were leery of the Anglos' separatist
tendencies. For this reason few tejanos openly backed the efforts of the Anglo colonists. Only one, Erasmo Seguín, signed
the petition for separation from Coahuila.

Stephen F. Austin was selected to travel to Mexico City to
present the convention's demands and its draft constitution to
the Mexican government. He left Texas in April 1833, one
month after Santa Anna and Gómez Farías were elected president and vice president of Mexico and a year before Santa
Anna's conversion to centralism. Austin was disturbed at the
growing rebelliousness of his fellow colonists and was at great
pains to assure the Mexicans that the Texans had no wish to
separate from Mexico.

Austin's trip was a fiasco. The journey to Mexico City took
three grueling months, culminating in a stagecoach journey
through Veracruz, which, in the summer of 1833, was a war
zone. Austin reached Mexico City in July, when the city was
in the grip of a full-blown cholera plague that would take
nearly twenty thousand lives in six weeks and afflict many
more, including Austin himself. Owing to the plague, congress recessed with no new session scheduled till late September. Upon Austin's arrival in Mexico City, President
Santa Anna was relaxing at his hacienda while Vice President
Valentín Gómez Farías made policy. Gómez Farías's reforms
had already begun ruffling feathers, and the seeds of new rebellions were beginning to sprout.

Still, Austin was optimistic for the most part. There was, in
fact, much sentiment in official circles in favor of granting the
Texans the reforms they requested, so Austin resolved to be
patient. But when congress finally reconvened in late September, it showed little interest in Texas. Around this same time
Austin learned that at least some impatient Texans were
planning to declare Texas's independence from Coahuila in

defiance of the law. Austin visited acting president Valentín
Gómez Farías and explained that the Texans would not toler-
ate much further delay. Gómez Farías was deeply angered by
what he interpreted as a threat, though Austin managed to explain that he was not advocating illegal actions but rather
merely reporting what was in fact already happening in Texas.
Gómez Farías appeared placated. Shortly after this meeting
Austin finally ran out of patience with the Mexican government's procrastination and wrote an angry and uncharacteris-
tically blunt letter to the *ayuntamiento* (city council) of San
Antonio. The Mexicans, he said, had no intention of doing
anything with respect to Texas, so Texans should take matters
into their own hands and organize a state government at
once. "There is no doubt," he wrote, "that the fate of Texas
depends upon itself and not upon this government."

By the end of 1833 prospects had brightened somewhat.
Although the machinery of the administration continued
moving at a glacial pace, in December congress finally approved the repeal of Article 11 of the Law of April 6, 1830.
The Coahuila legislature, at the urging of the central government, tried to placate the Texans by creating new munici-
palities and political departments and by giving them two
additional representatives in congress. It also passed a law
permitting the use of English in legal documents and decree-
ing that no one should be harassed for their religious views so
long as they did not disrupt public order. To top things off,
the state congress acceded to the Texan demands that appel-
late circuit courts be located in Texas and that citizens have
the right to trial by jury. It was reasonable to suppose that
Texas statehood was in the offing. Satisfied that the Mexican
and Coahuilan governments had now granted the Texans'
nearly every wish, and optimistic that Texas statehood would
not be long in coming, Austin set out for home.

Unfortunately for Austin, the city council at San Antonio
had been scandalized by his heated letter urging them to take

matters into their own hands: they had forwarded a copy of the seditious letter to the authorities in Mexico City. Gómez Farías was so enraged by this subversive conduct that he ordered Austin's arrest. Austin was taken into custody at Saltillo in early January 1834 and immediately returned to Mexico City, where for months he languished in a sixteen-by-thirteen-foot cell in an old Dominican monastery that had once housed prisoners of the Inquisition. The Mexicans were unable to agree on who had jurisdiction in Austin's case, so not only did the empresario not go to trial, he was never indicted, though he was held for nearly a year and a half. The tortuous letters he wrote from prison reveal just how puzzling Mexican politics of the day could be to one who had struggled so long to maintain a distance. "I have been true and faithful to this government and nation," he wrote, "have served them laboriously; have tried to do all the good I could to individuals and to the country; have been a philanthropist, and I am now meeting my reward. I expect to die in this prison."[6]

Austin's imprisonment was symptomatic of the Mexican government's deep and growing mistrust of the Anglo-Americans of Texas, even despite its willingness to make concessions on such matters as justice, slavery, tariffs, and immigration. In early 1834, at the same time Austin was being arrested in Saltillo, the Gómez Farías government sent a "fact-finding" mission to Coahuila and Texas. Colonel José María Noriega traveled to Monclova, which had replaced Saltillo as the capital of Coahuila and Texas in 1833, with orders to review all land transactions, reopen Texas customs houses, and identify Anglo-American troublemakers. Colonel Juan Nepomuceno Almonte was sent to Texas with orders to assure the Texans of the Mexican government's good intentions, while at the same time gauging the Texans' loyalty, tallying their numbers, investigating their access to arms and other martial resources, promising land grants to Indians, and cultivating loyal leaders. He was also ordered to find a way to alert the Texans' slaves to the fact that they were considered free under Mexican law and that they, together with freed slaves from the United States, were eligible for grants of vacant lands in Texas with which to form their own colonies. The Noriega-Almonte mission appeared to signal that the central government, even while granting many of the Texans' demands, planned to step up its efforts to bring Coahuila and Texas to heel. The mission likely gave the Texans cause to doubt the Mexican government's sincerity. In particular, the notion that blacks and Indians might be converted into a kind of fifth column for Mexico played into one of the Texas colonists' worst nightmares.

Even so, Colonel Almonte was able to report that Texas was quiet and the inhabitants apparently content. Such was not the case in Coahuila, where Colonel Noriega had to abandon his mission prematurely, fearing for his life. Coahuila's federalists were, for the moment, more assertive than their Texas counterparts. They refused to disband their volunteer militia when ordered to do so by the centralist army commander, Santa Anna's brother-in-law, General Martín Perfecto de Cos. They also desperately tried to increase the size of their militia by selling lands in Texas for bargain prices to charlatans who claimed they could raise an additional five hundred troops, causing outrage among the Texans. The conflict served to poison relations between the Texans and their fellow federalists in Coahuila, even while bringing the prospect of rebellion closer to home.

While Stephen Austin languished in Mexican prisons, back in Texas some frankly hoped the conciliatory empresario would not return. A split emerged between the old-guard conservatives like Austin, who wanted greater autonomy and a few administrative reforms, many of which had already been granted, and those who advocated independence and/or annexation to the United States. A large portion of the latter group was made up of recent arrivals who found that most of the best lands were taken, that prices were rising, and that their dreams of easy bounty would not be realized. The new-comers found it easy to blame Mexico for their disappoint-ments, and they began styling themselves the "war party," men who were eager to seize Texas from Mexico by any means necessary and who derided Stephen Austin and his ilk as "Tories." These people had little to lose and perhaps much to gain from a war.

Such was the situation that Austin confronted when, hav-ing been finally released from prison, he returned to Texas in September 1835. By that time events were moving in ways that clearly favored the position of the war party. Even though the Texans had recently been granted a number of special privileges, and those privileges had not been revoked, Santa Anna's move to quit the states of any semblance of au-tonomy outraged the Texans. While centralism was generally popular in the more central states, several peripheral states grew restive. In Zacatecas, Coahuila's neighbor to the south, radical federalist governor Francisco García had long been a thorn in the side of the central authorities. García had built up the largest civic militia in Mexico, and his government had carried out a number of bold experiments without the bless-ings of Mexico City. García was the most progressive gover-nor of his day, but unfortunately his military skills fell short of his administrative skills. When he rebelled against the Santa Anna regime in the spring of 1835, Santa Anna came out of yet another bout of semiretirement on his hacienda to lead a force northward, decisively crushing García's forces in a two-hour battle in which some two thousand were killed. After-ward Santa Anna authorized the brutal ransacking of the city of Zacatecas and the looting of the state's rich silver mines. The extreme cruelty of the assault added some luster to Santa Anna's reputation among those disposed to admire such res-oluteness, but all who favored federalism were understand-ably alarmed.

Stephen F. Austin was disillusioned with Santa Anna, and he was also angry at having suffered a long imprisonment by a government he had staked his reputation to defend. Austin now declared himself finished with conciliatory measures. "I am tired of this government," he wrote. "They are always in revolution and I believe always will be." By the autumn of 1835 Austin had gone decisively over to the war party.

In late June 1835 a prominent member of the war party named William Barret Travis, a lawyer who had entered Texas illegally in 1831 after killing a man in Alabama, led an impetuous attack on the customs house and military garrison at Anáhuac. Many of his fellow citizens denounced him as a hothead and reaffirmed their allegiance to Mexico, but rumors swirled that Santa Anna was bent on a military occupation of Texas, and the Texans began war preparations. In September, Colonel Domingo de Ugartechea, who commanded the San Antonio garrison, sent a detachment to the village of Gonzales to demand that the villagers there surrender a cannon that had been provided them to fend off hostile Indians. The villagers refused to surrender the cannon, resulting in a small skirmish on October 2, 1835. The Anglo citizens hurriedly formed a Texas "Army of the People," choosing Stephen F. Austin as commander in chief, and the Texas Revolution was under way.

Santa Anna was determined to make an example of the Texans. Brutality had worked rather well for him in the siege of Zacatecas in May, and a decisive trouncing of the Texans would further burnish his heroic credentials. Upon setting out in November 1835, Santa Anna declared, with typical bombast, that it had been years since he had seen "in the Republic a body of troops more brilliant in their discipline and equipment nor more uniform in their opinion and enthusiasm."[7] Santa Anna evidently had a monumental capacity to delude himself and others, for in fact the army he led to Texas was made up of the rawest recruits gathered unwillingly from populations of vagabonds, Indians, and criminals. The rebellions of 1832 and 1833 had left the regular army—a fairly haphazard force to begin with—in disarray, and there had not been time to reorganize and rebuild. So little money was available for the expedition that Santa Anna had to mortgage his own properties and contract ruinous loans to buy supplies. The army had little food, ragged clothing, antiquated equipment, practically no medicine or trained doctors, and primitive weapons left over from colonial times. Although most of the army was comprised of infantry required to march across hundreds of miles of rugged terrain, the soldiers lacked even adequate footwear. There was a shortage of mules, so the army had to make do with lumbering oxen, many of whom perished from fatigue on the long journey and were left to rot, their meat unfit for human consumption. Santa Anna's army had to live off the land, but the land was stingy and capricious. No rain fell in December, and lack of water was a severe problem. The deserts were dry and barren of grass for the horses, and the wild fruits the soldiers devoured caused a plague of dysentery. January and February were bitter cold, something soldiers from the tropics were ill prepared to endure. The Mexican army was further slowed and weakened by the large number of camp followers—wives and relatives of the soldiers—who tagged along. For reasons that are unclear, Santa Anna appears to have assumed that the Indians of Texas would side with the Mexicans, but the Indians favored neither one side nor the other. They attacked frequently, especially in the area south of the Rio Grande, and stole foodstuffs that had been stored for the army on small ranches before the soldiers arrived. Nor did the impoverished local Mexican population provide much support.

The Texas Army of the People was not especially impressive either. Like the Mexican force, the Texan army was poorly supplied, and desertion and indiscipline were chronic problems. But most of the Texan soldiers were highly motivated, and they had not endured a forced march through an unforgiving desert. Volunteers were promised at least 640 acres of land as a reward should the Texans prevail, a more powerful incentive than anything the Mexican soldiers could claim. And many of the Texan troops were fighting on their own turf, whereas the Mexicans were six hundred miles from home. The Texans also had an ample supply of long rifles, while the Mexicans had to make do with smoothbore muskets that had less than half the effective range. The Texans were badly outnumbered, but that disadvantage, as it turned out, did not doom their cause.

While Santa Anna and his army were en route, the Texans made some gains. In November they held a convention, which formed a provisional government officially called the Consultation, the authority of which was a bit ambiguous. The Consultation tried to reconcile the competing war and peace factions by refusing to declare Texas independence (officially this rebellion was to be for the restoration of the federalist Constitution of 1824), even while naming as governor Henry Smith, a leader of the war party and a longtime advocate of independence who openly despised Mexicans. The Texans managed to seize the lightly defended fortress at Goliad in October, and in December a Texan force dislodged General Cos's troops from San Antonio. Sam Houston replaced Austin as military chief, while Austin was detailed to head a commission to the United States to seek money, military supplies, diplomatic support, and recruits for the Texas army. The commission was also instructed to sound out U.S. authorities on the issue of annexing Texas to the United States.

The almost effortless expulsion of the Mexican centralists from San Antonio had made the Texans overconfident, for most of those who participated in the action congratulated themselves and went home. San Antonio was situated on the Old San Antonio Road, one of only two important roads passing from Mexico through Texas, and it was home to a *presidio* (fortress), an old fortified mission known as the Alamo. The other road, known as the Atascosito Road, ran from Matamoros on the Rio Grande up to Austin's San Felipe colony. That road was guarded by the Presidio La Bahia at Goliad. The Texans occupied both fortresses, but when the first wave of volunteers scattered, the fortresses were held by very slender contingents who were poorly armed and lacking basic provisions and whose main hope lay in newly arrived volunteers from the United States. It was commonly acknowledged that neither fort could be long defended against a sustained siege. Sam Houston, commander in chief of the Texas Army of the People, advocated abandoning the Alamo and blowing it up, and then concentrating the Texas forces in East Texas, where the Anglo-Americans were more numerous and new arrivals from across the U.S. border more likely to appear. He was overruled by Governor Smith, who unwisely believed the Alamo could be held.

Santa Anna entered San Antonio on February 23 with some 2,500 weary troops. The gathering threat emboldened the Texans, who on March 2, at a convention at the town of Washington-on-the-Brazos, formally declared their independence from Mexico. In San Antonio the odds were grim for the Texans, who were determined to defend the Alamo with only 150 men and whatever reinforcements might appear before the Mexicans cut off all access. The defenders answered Santa Anna's surrender demand with a cannon shot. The Mexicans then commenced artillery bombardment of the fort, reducing the walls to rubble. The defenders sent desperate calls for reinforcements, but only thirty-two troops from Gonzales answered the call. On March 5, after twelve days of shelling, Santa Anna announced he would begin an assault. This announcement took his officers by surprise, since the rebels clearly had no hope of being reinforced and were nearly out of provisions: their surrender could not possibly be far off. Since the fort's defenders had a variety of artillery pieces, a siege would inevitably be costly for the Mexican forces. Moreover, the Alamo was of marginal strategic importance, as the rebels' stronghold was in East Texas, and the Presidio La Bahia at Goliad was the gateway to that region. This wanton recklessness likely was inspired by Santa Anna's desire to avenge the Texans' victory at San Antonio in December, when his brother-in-law, General Cos, had been forced to retreat across the Rio Grande. Santa Anna hoped to take the Alamo and report his glorious feat to Mexico City, where military victories made up so much of his political capital. He also hoped to send a menacing message to the rebels. Apparently he thought this worth the sacrifice of several hundred lives.

The assault began before dawn on Sunday, March 6. About 1800 Mexican troops stormed the fort from four directions, to be immediately decimated and driven back by deadly artillery and rifle fire. But eventually the Mexicans' superior numbers proved decisive. In little more than an hour all of the Alamo's defenders—whose numbers are variously estimated at between 189 and 257—had died in combat or been summarily executed in its aftermath. Perhaps 600 Mexicans were killed in the battle.

Five days later Sam Houston arrived at Gonzales to organize the relief of the Alamo, finding only 300 men gathered there for that purpose. The same day he received word that the Alamo had fallen, its defenders slaughtered. Uneager to face the Mexicans with so small a force, Houston prudently ordered a retreat to East Texas. That left civilian settlements of central Texas vulnerable to the depredations of Santa Anna's marauding army, causing panicked settlers to torch their homes and flee for dear life, an episode known to Texas history as the Runaway Scrape. Colonel James Fannin, who had been biding his time at the Goliad presidio, was keenly aware that his poorly armed contingent of around 300 men was no match for the Mexicans. On March 20 he negotiated a surrender agreement wherein his men were promised treatment as prisoners of war. The Mexican commander, the relatively humane General José de Urrea, assured Fannin that Santa Anna would grant them clemency. Fannin and his men were held for a time at the La Bahia fortress at Goliad. Another group of rebels numbering around 80 surrendered to Urrea under the same terms on March 22. Urrea recommended to Santa Anna that his assurances of clemency be honored; Santa Anna replied with orders that all prisoners should be executed at once. On March 27, Palm Sunday, the prisoners were divided into three groups and marched out of the presidio at Goliad. They were told various stories about the purpose of this march but were given no cause to suspect treachery. A short way out of town the columns were halted, and at a prearranged signal, the guards began shooting the prisoners at close range. At least 342 men were murdered and their bodies burned.

Santa Anna's own glorified reports of his triumphs were playing well back in Mexico City. Pro–Santa Anna newspapers abandoned all restraint, insisting their man's deeds had exceeded those of Alexander the Great and Napoleon and suggesting with little subtlety that he be made supreme dictator, perhaps even king. But Santa Anna's butcheries at the Alamo and Goliad had quite a different impact in Texas and the United States, where they reinforced the image of Mexican tyranny and Anglo gallantry and galvanized the will to resist. Even Stephen Austin, who had long presented himself as Mexico's most faithful servant, could not resist indulging in racist diatribes. In a widely publicized letter of May 4, he wrote that a "war of extermination is raging in Texas, a war of barbarism and of despotic principles, waged by the mongrel Spanish-Indian and Negro race, against civilization and the Anglo-American race."[8] The notion that white Anglo-Saxons represented civilization while other races were its foes was already a staple of U.S. discourse, but the brutality of Santa Anna's Texas campaign helped to solidify that notion, and relations between Anglo-Americans and Mexicans deteriorated accordingly.

Santa Anna apparently believed that the Battle of the Alamo had ended the war, and he only reluctantly allowed his officers to persuade him that mopping-up operations against Sam Houston's army were necessary. He divided his forces into three parts. His own contingent moved eastward while Houston retreated till he and his army of perhaps nine hundred men reached Lynch's Ferry on the San Jacinto River. There Houston's forces surprised the Mexicans on April 21, decisively routing them in a somewhat anticlimactic twenty-minute battle. Virtually all of the soldiers of Santa Anna's army—some thirteen hundred men—were either killed, captured, or forced to flee. Santa Anna escaped but was captured the following day. Considerable clamor arose for his immediate execution, but instead he was made to sign two treaties, one of which was made public, the other kept secret. In the public treaty Santa Anna conceded that the war was over and vowed that the Mexican army would stay south of the Rio Grande, never again to make war against Texas. Mexican troops, according to the treaty, were to evacuate Texas, respecting property and returning or paying for any that they confiscated or destroyed. The secret treaty said that Santa Anna was free to return home on the condition that he see to it that Mexico officially recognize the independence of Texas.

Although it was not altogether apparent at the time, the treaty negotiated between the victorious Texans and General Santa Anna included a provision that would become a vital spark igniting Mexico's war with the United States. The treaty claimed the Rio Grande (or Río Bravo del Norte, as it was known in Mexico) as the new republic's southern boundary, a provision that was nothing less than an audacious land grab by the Texans. The Mexican state of Texas had always

been bounded to the south by the Nueces River. The area between the Rio Grande and Nueces Rivers—an arid, nearly
worthless, impoverished, sparsely inhabited tract of land—
would become the source of enormous contention between
Texas, the United States, and Mexico.

The treaties were signed on May 14, 1836. The meaning
of the Texas Revolution has been debated ever since that
time. For generations, the most widely accepted view in the
United States has held that this was a revolution against
tyranny and oppression, waged by a people who found themselves culturally and politically incompatible with their rulers.
A variation on this theme holds that the Texans simply lost
patience with the factionalism and chronic upheavals of Mexican politics. Neither of these explanations is entirely con-
vincing.

There is no question that Santa Anna was a tyrant, but for
the Texas colonists "tyranny" was an uncommonly broad category. It included, for example, the government's efforts to
collect tariffs. And yet as General Terán wearily reminded
Stephen Austin after colonists attacked the Texas customs
houses in 1832, "customs duties [are] paid from Hudson's Bay
to the Horn, and only at Brazoria [are] they considered cause
for violence."[9] "Tyranny" also included the Mexican government's efforts to eradicate slavery, which the Texans insisted
was crucial to their economic survival; efforts to impose a
common system of justice throughout the republic; religious
intolerance (which was never enforced in Texas); attempts
to control immigration into Mexico; and the attachment
of Texas to the state of Coahuila.

The Mexican government, eager to see the colonization of
Texas work, sought to placate the Texans by giving in to all of
their demands except that they be made a separate state. By
any reckoning, the Texans were Mexico's most privileged citizens. The notion that the Texans resorted to rebellion only
after long years of enduring Mexican oppression is further

undercut by the fact that the most vociferous advocates of rebellion in Texas were people who arrived there after 1830, many of them entering the state illegally. Nearly a third of the Texas independence fighters showed up only after war had already begun. Many of them were, in the words of San Antonio political chief Ramón Múzquiz, "violent and desperate men who have nothing to lose."[10]

The argument that the Texans rebelled because they could no longer endure the chronic factionalism and political instability in central Mexico cannot be glibly dismissed. After all, Stephen Austin did make a sincere effort to be a good citizen of Mexico and to persuade his colonists to do likewise. Only after repeated frustrations and a lengthy imprisonment did he embrace rebellion. And yet it is also true that Texas itself was part and parcel of Mexico's instability. The centrifugal tendencies of Mexico's regions contributed enormously to Mexico's political troubles, and no state agitated more forcefully for its right to ignore the dictates of the central government than Texas. As of 1832, the Texans became full-fledged participants in Mexico's instability by joining Santa Anna's federalist revolt against the central government. Moreover, the Texans' exasperation at Mexico's political instability rings hollow when one considers the government of the independent republic of Texas, which would prove every bit as unstable and riven by faction as that of Mexico. Indeed, bitter factionalism was evident in Texas long before the Texas rebellion commenced.

The issue that finally provoked the colonists to rebellion— the revocation of states' rights under the centralist regime of 1835—was unpopular with most of the peripheral states and provoked several rebellions, but only in Texas did rebellion result in a complete break with Mexico. There were rebellions in the northern states of New Mexico, Sonora, and California, but those rebellions played out with dramatically different results. At least in part because Anglo-Americans with close connections to the United States participated only marginally in those rebellions, the Mexican government took a more conciliatory approach, even to the point of recognizing an outspoken federalist as governor of California.

Texas was truly a special case, one that cannot be divorced from the general context of U.S.-Mexican relations. The United States gave the Mexicans every reason to fear treachery in Texas, for it did not bother to disguise its wish to acquire Texas by any means. As General Terán had pointed out back in 1832, there was reason to suspect that the United States was engineering a replay of its acquisition of West Florida, with Americans flooding into a coveted territory, then striking up a chorus of complaints, "assuming rights . . . which it is impossible to sustain in a serious discussion," eventually leading to rebellion and a period of independence followed by annexation to the United States. The Mexicans were inspired to take such forceful measures against the Texas rebellion by a well-justified anxiety.

Ironically, it was Santa Anna's cruelty and military ineptitude that hastened the loss of Texas. That loss would become, in the minds of many Mexican leaders, a festering wound, an affront to the national honor that had to be avenged at any cost.

5

THE ELUSIVE RECONQUEST

After his humiliating defeat at San Jacinto, it appeared certain that Santa Anna's career had come to a crushing, ignominious end. But the perpetual dysfunction of the Mexican government, combined with a remarkable series of events, brought him once again to power. This time he would abandon all restraint, indulging his every debauched and vainglorious whim. Among those whims was the commissioning of a gilt-bronze statue of himself pointing defiantly northward, toward Texas. His detractors noted that the statue was also pointing in the direction of the mint, but the message Santa Anna wished to convey was clear: he, Santa Anna, was the man—the only man—who could carry out the ardently desired re-conquest of the lost province.

Politicians decreed that the loss of Texas was a blight upon the nation's honor and that recapturing that province was the primary national imperative. Unfortunately, they spent little time pondering the true reasons for the loss of Texas, choosing to blame that loss on the perfidy of the United States and of their own political rivals rather than on Mexico's weakness. Analyzing and addressing the root causes of Mexico's weakness was obviously a difficult task. The ambitious politicos of the 1830s and 1840s found it easier and more profitable to seize on the Texas issue as fodder in demagogic campaigns. The loss of Texas added still more poison to the already toxic brew that was Mexican politics.

SANTA ANNA RETURNS

Although Mexican politicians insisted that reconquering Texas was well within the realm of possibility, optimism in general had come to seem a dangerous delusion during the 1830s. The chambers where congress met seemed a microcosm of the country at large: thieves had stolen lead from the building's roof, and water would pour in from the daily torrents that pelted the highlands in winter, soiling carpets, books, and papers and leaving a heavy, depressing stench. Outside those chambers the scene was grimmer still: the rain caused raw sewage to overflow into streets teeming with beggars and bandits. There was a police force, but due to chronic budget shortfalls they were rarely paid and were ever receptive to bribes from criminals. Even those few criminals who were arrested found it easy enough to escape and could just as easily disappear into the army, where they were welcomed warmly.

The spring of 1835 brought Santa Anna's vainglorious accounts of his triumphs over the Texans, and that lightened the mood as his admirers took the occasion to compose patriotic songs and poems in his honor and to portray him once again as the nation's savior. But in May that triumph seemed a cruel joke, as news arrived of Santa Anna's defeat at the Battle of San Jacinto and his capitulation to the Texans. The acting president ordered that all flags be flown at half-staff and all military standards be draped in mourning. At Santa Anna's orders, the remaining Mexican troops in Texas began their

"Mexico is the country of inequality," wrote the German scientist Alexander von Humboldt. The point is borne out in this lithograph by the Italian artist Claudio Linati, who published his observations of Mexico's land and people in 1828.

Agustín de Iturbide, the royalist military officer who secured Mexico's independence in 1821, and was crowned emperor of Mexico in 1822

Stephen F. Austin, the most successful of the Texas *empresarios*. His motto was "Fidelity to Mexico."

Joel Roberts Poinsett, first U.S. ambassador to Mexico. A zealous advocate of liberal ideas and institutions, he was accused by critics of meddling in Mexico's domestic affairs.

General Manuel de Mier y Terán, who led the fact-finding mission to Texas in 1828–29, and later tried to implement the Law of April 6, 1830, as commandant of the Eastern Interior Provinces. Despondent over the failures of Mexican policy, he committed suicide in 1832.

General Vicente Guerrero. A man of mixed race, a committed liberal, and a hero of the wars of independence, he seized the presidency in 1828, was ousted in 1829, and rebelled in 1831.

General Antonio López de Santa Anna, Mexico's great caudillo

Valentín Gómez Farías. Santa Anna's vice president in 1833–34 and again in 1846–47, he was a leader of the *puro* liberal faction and a leading advocate of war with the United States.

General Anastasio Bustamante, conservative leader who served as president on three occasions

General José Joaquín de Herrera. President of Mexico in 1844–45, he was a moderate leader who tried to ease tensions with the United States before being overthrown by Mariano Paredes y Arrillaga. He would regain his office in 1848.

General Mariano Paredes y Arrillaga. An avowed monarchist, he overthrew the government of José Joaquín de Herrera on the eve of hostilities with the United States, charging that Herrera was insufficiently bellicose.

President James K. Polk, President of the United States, 1845–49. An ardent expansionist, he was determined to gain Mexico's northern territories for the United States.

The storming of Chapultepec, as depicted by the German artist Carl Nebel

Nicholas Trist, who ignored a recall order from Polk in order to complete the negotiations ending the war

Monument to the Niños Heroes, the heroic cadets who, according to legend, fought to the death rather than surrender Chapultepec Castle to the American invaders. The monument, which was inaugurated in 1952, contains the remains of the cadets. PHOTOGRAPH BY JÜRGEN BUCHENAU

retreat, despite the misgivings of their commander, General Vicente Filisola. As if to add a cruel flourish to the Mexicans' disgrace, the Texas skies opened and rain drenched the dispirited retreating soldiers, forcing them to slog through the black muddy prairies of South Texas clutching what few miserable items they had managed to plunder along the way.

In Mexico City the conservative General Anastasio Bustamante was elected president in April 1836 to an eight-year term. His first act in office was to revoke all legislation decreed by Santa Anna and to disavow the treaties Santa Anna had signed with the Texans. Santa Anna's disgrace was nearly total. In the place of comparisons to Napoleon came comparisons to Nero; rather than being celebrated as the savior of the nation, he was denounced as a vile traitor. In his defense Santa Anna later noted that he had signed those treaties with the Texans in his own name, not that of the Mexican nation. He had, he argued, fully intended that the nation should disavow those agreements.

Santa Anna was held for a time by the Texans, many of whom strongly favored his execution. President Andrew Jackson intervened in the matter, counseling his protégé Sam Houston that Santa Anna had great value as a captive, since the Mexican army—which was even then regrouping at Matamoros—would hesitate to invade Texas as long as their erstwhile leader was in chains. During the months of Santa Anna's captivity the U.S. Congress debated whether to recognize the new Republic of Texas. Some congressmen argued that to do so would risk angering Mexico, so Sam Houston conceived the idea of sending General Santa Anna to Washington, D.C., where he could meet personally with President Jackson and assure him that Mexico had no intention of reconquering Texas. In November Santa Anna was sent overland to Washington, through a country teeming with people who considered him an archfiend worthy of assassination. After his meeting with President Jackson, Santa Anna was placed aboard a ship for Veracruz, where he arrived in February 1837, to be met by a tepid crowd that only watched in gloomy silence as the salute was given and the band began to play. Santa Anna returned to his sprawling estate to enjoy another bucolic retirement.

Mexico could surely have benefited from strong, decisive leadership during these troubled times. The freshly elected president, Anastasio Bustamante, did not supply it. Although his earlier administration, which had governed from 1830 to 1832, could claim some positive accomplishments, he was generally seen as hopelessly irresolute, albeit honest and sincere. One of his severest critics, Carlos Bustamante (no relation), charged that he had never bothered to read the new constitution he was sworn to uphold.

Bustamante faced daunting problems. For Mexican patriots of the 1830s, the loss of Texas was far more than a loss of real estate: it was a deep wound to the national honor. That a handful of ruffians in a far-off province could have inflicted terrible losses on the Mexican army and wrested the province away by themselves was too painful to admit. The conviction grew that the Texans had been nothing more or less than the agents of a U.S. conspiracy against Mexico. Heated denunciations of the Americans became standard fare in Mexican political discourse, and the need to avenge this hideous injustice became a national imperative. Naturally, the only institution in Mexico capable of exacting that revenge was the army, which invariably was given top priority in budgeting decisions. But by 1837 the treasury was running an annual deficit of eighteen million pesos, and the government had no collateral left. Bustamante soon discovered that, for all the ardent demands that Texas be reconquered, no one was anxious to finance the venture. Bustamante's every effort to find funding ended up alienating one or another of the very constituencies he relied upon to uphold his government. When he pressured the church to make its property available as collateral for public loans, the church countered by selling off its assets. When he instituted new "emergency" taxes on the wealthy, the wealthy grumbled and threatened rebellion.

Meanwhile, federalists took some delight in the government's woes, for they placed much of the blame for Mexico's humiliation squarely on the shoulders of the centralists. The Texans, after all, had rebelled against centralism, which as far as the federalists were concerned proved positively that centralism was hastening the disintegration of the nation. Federalists rebelled in other parts of the country as well, forcing the government to expend still more resources in defeating them. When Valentín Gómez Farías—for conservatives, the archfiend of radical federalism—returned to Mexico from exile in early 1838, the federalist threat appeared to grow more menacing. Demands for the restoration of the federalist Constitution of 1824 led to riots and demonstrations in the streets of Mexico City. It was at this point that the Supreme Conservative Power—the institution that had been created to mediate disputes between the government's various branches—declared that if the Bustamante government could not hold the line, then emergency powers should be granted to none other than Antonio López de Santa Anna.

The surprising political rehabilitation of Santa Anna was made possible by other, unrelated events that were culminating that same winter of 1838. For some years France had been complaining that its citizens suffered enormously from the violence and poverty of Mexico and was demanding payment for their losses. The Mexicans resisted those demands, pointing out that of the six-hundred thousand pesos France was demanding, a whopping sixty thousand were claimed by a single pastry chef from Veracruz to compensate him for the destruction of a shop that was in fact valued at less than a thousand pesos. When the Mexican congress rejected a French ultimatum, French warships blockaded the port of Veracruz, and the so-called Pastry War was under way.

In Mexico City government propaganda tried to stir up popular hysteria by conjuring the specter of a full-scale international war that could result in still further dismemberment. The presence with the fleet of the twenty-year-old Prince de Joinville, son of the French king Louis Philippe, inspired rumors that the French meant to impose a monarch upon Mexico. On November 27 the French bombarded the old fortress of San Juan de Ullua. President Bustamante issued a draconian order that all men capable of bearing arms be immediately conscripted. When the military commanders at San Juan de Ullua and Veracruz, feeling themselves outgunned, surrendered to the French, the government relieved them of their command and, with many misgivings, placed General Santa Anna, the caudillo of Veracruz, in charge.

With characteristic energy, Santa Anna assembled an ad hoc army and rushed to the city to attack the French. The French fired a captured cannon loaded with grapeshot, killing Santa Anna's horse from under him and wounding him severely in his arm and leg. The next day doctors studied the leg wound and declared the appendage could not be saved. They amputated the limb with excruciating ineptitude. Santa Anna seized the occasion to indulge his love of melodramatic self-aggrandizement, composing a deathbed message celebrating the "last victory I offer my country." He asked that Mexicans forget his political mistakes and remember him only as "a good Mexican."

It did not matter that this was in no sense a "victory"—in fact, the dispute with the French was eventually resolved through negotiation, in which the Mexicans agreed to nearly all of the French demands. It was enough that Santa Anna had *claimed* victory and, more important, that he had sacrificed a body part in defense of the fatherland. Both Santa Anna and his severed leg were carried to Manga de Clavo, where the general began a remarkably rapid convalescence. He was, once again, hailed as a great hero, the savior of the fatherland. This stunning political rehabilitation said much about the dysfunctional condition of Mexico's politics. As Bustamante's government appeared to be flailing helplessly, more and more people were concluding that power should be placed in the hands of a proven man of action. Santa Anna was, as ever, eager to oblige.

In July 1840 Mexico City experienced the most violent coup attempt in its history, this one led by Gómez Farías against Bustamante. For nearly two weeks cannon and rifle fire shook the city, destroying much property and littering downtown streets with dead and wounded people who were left to the mercy of ravenous wild dogs. Bustamante's government survived the coup, but the violence of the attempt profoundly shocked the polite society of the capital and turned many people against both Bustamante and his federalist adversaries.

In October, Mexico City society was shaken by the appearance of a pamphlet arguing that Mexico's only hope lay in reestablishing a monarchy under a prince from a European royal house. Its author, José María Gutiérrez de Estrada, was mercilessly attacked and hounded into exile for advocating such a scandalous view, but the very heatedness of the response was indicative of the depths of Mexico's political crisis: many people by now were convinced that the politicians would always make a hash of things and that perhaps monarchy was worth another look.

In August 1841 General Mariano Paredes—a hard-drinking, hard-gambling, archreactionary, and notoriously ambitious former royalist officer who openly favored monarchy—rebelled against Bustamante from Guadalajara. This was something new: a centralist revolt against a centralist government. The rebellion rocked Mexico City at the same time that a series of earth tremors and vicious thunderstorms struck, heightening the pervasive sense of dread. In mid-September Santa Anna joined the rebellion, leading his troops into Mexico City from the east while General Paredes came from the west, joining General Gabriel Valencia, who led the revolt within the capital. The generals dissolved the government and empowered Santa Anna to appoint a committee to find a provisional president. Santa Anna, to no one's surprise, appointed himself to the job.

In March and April 1842 elections were held to form a new congress. Santa Anna decreed that these elections should be founded on universal male suffrage—no literacy tests, no property or income qualifications. The vote turned out in fact to be a resounding endorsement of federalism, but by the time the liberal congressmen took their seats, Santa Anna was behaving very much like a king. Congress nevertheless set about producing a new constitution while Santa Anna bided his time at Manga de Clavo. The constitution they wrote was by far the most liberal one Mexico had seen, going so far as to decree—in addition, of course, to federalism—religious tolerance, an end to special privileges, universal male suffrage, free public education, and guaranteed civil rights for all. But this was all a charade: no sooner had congress released its draft constitution than the army dissolved congress and replaced it with a committee of wealthy and conservative men. The committee then wrote a very conservative and centralist constitution, known as the Organic Bases, that did not mention civil rights and that once again restricted political participation to the wealthy.

The new constitution was approved on Santa Anna's birthday, which was lavishly celebrated with Te Deums, specially commissioned dramas, songs of praise to the nation's hero, and a six-thousand-man military parade through the streets of Mexico City. There were bullfights and fireworks and at one point the bizarre spectacle of Santa Anna, the wealthy provisional president of a starving country, standing on the balcony of the National Palace tossing specially minted five-hundred-peso silver coins to the crowd below.

Still gaudier spectacles soon followed, for Santa Anna was

thoroughly intoxicated with the outward trappings of power. Construction was begun on a new Santa Anna Theatre, statues were erected, and medals were struck declaring Santa Anna "Benefactor of the Fatherland," "Hero of Independence," and even "Founder of the Republic." The most curious episode came in September when, on the anniversary of Santa Anna's victory over the French at Tampico, Santa Anna had an elaborate burial ceremony performed for his amputated leg. The shriveled appendage was carried from his Veracruz hacienda in a splendid coach, paraded through the streets of the capital, placed in an enormous urn, and laid to rest in a small mausoleum in central Mexico City, solemnly eulogized with speeches, songs, and poems. In public appearances Santa Anna was invariably introduced by beating drums and blaring trumpets and was always surrounded by pompous generals and retainers decked out in resplendent scarlet and gold uniforms. His own blue and red uniform was richly embroidered with gold.

The new constitution prepared the way for elections at the end of 1843, which Santa Anna won handily. With that the Mexican Republic was effectively destroyed, and Santa Anna had attained something his enemies had long dreaded and that he and his diehard supporters had long hoped for. In the words of Fanny Calderón de la Barca: "Let all this end as it may, let them give everything whatever name is most popular, the government is now a military dictatorship."[1]

THE REPUBLIC OF TEXAS

Mexico surely had its share of problems, but its wayward former state of Texas had no cause to gloat. Although its population nearly doubled in its first four years as a republic, it remained sparsely populated, with only about 55,000 non-Indian people in a territory of some 250,000 square miles. (By contrast, the largest U.S. state, Virginia, was one-fourth the size but had twenty times the number of inhabitants.) About 8,000 of its people were slaves.

The Texas Republic's first president, Sam Houston, complained at the start of his term that the country's finances "have been in a more embarrassed situation doubtless than any other nation has ever experienced."[2] The Texas treasury held only five hundred dollars, and the provisional government that had overseen the revolution against Mexico bequeathed the new republic a debt of one and a quarter-million dollars. Soldiers and public servants went unpaid, and there seemed little hope of improvement. Politicians placed great stock in the notion that Texas's abundant public lands would be its financial salvation, but those lands were entirely undeveloped, and few roads connected them to potential markets. Moreover, Texas came into existence at a moment when the United States—the most likely source of land buyers—was itself plunged into a dire financial panic. Land speculators found that improved lands within the United States could be bought for a song, so the wild lands of Texas were easy to resist.

Nor was Texas able to secure loans. The British refused even to recognize the republic until November 1840. Recognition faced heated opposition from Britain's abolitionists, as well as from financiers who held unredeemed Mexican bonds and who feared that becoming cozy with Texas might anger the Mexicans and further dim their chances of ever seeing repayment. The British also noted that Texas's very existence as a sovereign republic was uncertain: it could conceivably be reconquered by Mexico or annexed by the United States. Prospective loans from French banks fell through because the French government, having scant faith that Texas could maintain its sovereignty, refused to back those loans. Mexico's refusal either to recognize Texas's independence or to formally end hostilities was an enormous obstacle to the republic's diplomatic and financial success. The only loans Texas

was able to secure carried ruinous terms, made still more ruinous by the republic's inevitable default on payments. The
public debt soared from one and a quarter-million dollars at
independence to nearly a billion ten years later. In desperation, the government of Texas issued paper money, which of
course depreciated rapidly till, by 1840, bills were worth no
more than twenty cents to the dollar.

The Texans were especially dismayed by the attitude of the
United States. Many Texans had assumed that once they had
declared their independence from Mexico, annexation to the
United States would be practically automatic. Stephen F.
Austin, with impressive prescience, had believed otherwise.
The question of annexation, he wrote, would provoke violent
opposition from northern antislavery forces, who would see it
as a southern plot to increase their voting power by adding a
new slave state. "Threats and denunciations . . . will goad the
North into a determined opposition and if Texas is annexed at
all it will not be until the question has convulsed this nation
for several sessions of Congress."[3] Even Andrew Jackson, Sam
Houston's old friend and mentor who had never made a secret of his wish to acquire Texas, dragged his feet on the issue.
The end of his presidential term coincided with the Texas
Revolution, which he denounced as "rash and premature."
He did not wish to saddle his handpicked successor, Martin
Van Buren, with a ferocious controversy; nor was he eager to
risk war with Mexico or to alienate the European powers,
who would surely resent too rapid movement toward acquiring Texas. The United States did not formally recognize the
Republic of Texas until March 1837, nearly a year after the
Battle of San Jacinto, and the question of annexation was
placed on indefinite hold. An official request from Texas for
annexation in August 1837 was rebuffed, and the following
year the Texans voted to withdraw their petition. Radical expansionists in the United States, meanwhile, began to work
feverishly to devise some rationale for Texas annexation that

would please North and South, abolitionist and slaveholder alike.

Much depended on Mexico's attitude, which remained implacably hostile toward Texas. The Texans—or at least those who were inclined to take a conciliatory course—embarked on a bumpy journey in search of an "honorable peace" with Mexico, in the hope that recognition by Mexico would improve their standing in the concert of nations. The effort was hindered by several factors that would prove insurmountable. The Texans insisted that Mexico's recognition of Texas's independence be full and unconditional and that the Mexicans acknowledge the republic's southern boundary to be the Rio Grande, not the Nueces River. Mexican politicians were practically unanimous in their conviction that agreeing to such terms would stain the nation's honor and be politically suicidal. The Mexicans insisted that the southern boundary of Texas must be the Nueces River, and that the lands between the Rio Grande and the Nueces should form a buffer zone to protect Mexico against Texas or U.S. aggression.

On the other side, a substantial portion of the Texas population had no desire for good relations with Mexico but instead clamored for war and the seizure of additional Mexican territory. "Texas proper is bounded by the Rio Grande," wrote the bellicose vice president of Texas, David G. Burnet. "Texas as defined by the sword, may comprehend the Sierra Madre. Let the sword do its proper work."[4] Given such attitudes, the prospect of bargaining in good faith was farfetched from the outset.

Although rumors of a formidable Mexican military effort at reconquest were a staple of Texas discourse, and although the Mexicans talked incessantly and collected taxes on the pretext of funding such an effort, the actual threat was remote. The Mexican army remained poorly armed and supplied, top heavy with officers who had advanced through political connections rather than military competence, and

manned by impoverished, undisciplined, and unwilling conscripts. Mexican hopes for an anti-Texas alliance with the
Cherokee Indians fell through when one Manuel Flores, who
was presumed to be a bandit with a gang of Cherokee allies,
was killed by Texas troops in May 1839. On Flores's body was
found a diary revealing that he was in fact operating at the be-
hest of the Mexican government in hopes of forging a broad
Mexican-Cherokee alliance against the Texans. The discovery
provided Mirabeau Buonaparte Lamar, Texas president from
December 1838 till December 1841, the pretext he sought to
make war without quarter against the Cherokees, eliminating
any threat they might have posed.

The Texas government alternated hostile policies toward
Mexico with attempts at diplomacy. British bondholders, still
awaiting repayment of loans made to Mexico in the early days
of the republic, hatched a scheme to coax the Mexicans into
feeling more warmly toward Texas. According to this scheme,
the Texas government would grant the British bondholders
some $5 million worth of Texas public lands; in return, the
bondholders would agree to forgive an equal amount of Mexico's debt on the condition that Mexico recognize Texas's independence. But not even the prospect of fiscal relief could
induce the Mexicans to deal with the Texans. One Texas
diplomat, James Treat, went to Mexico in December 1839
hoping to negotiate peace. He arrived to find the Mexican
congress considering a proposal to raise emergency taxes to
make war against Texas, and another proposal to charge anyone who spoke favorably about Texas with treason—not en-
couraging signs. He spent a frustrating and fruitless nine
months in Mexico before finally requesting his passports.

While true peace between Texas and Mexico was unlikely,
war seemed a perpetual possibility. The centralist governments of Bustamante and Santa Anna were plagued by periodic federalist rebellions, and the Texans did not always resist
the temptation to aid and abet those uprisings. In 1839 rebels

in Mexico's northern states declared their independence from Mexico, forming their own Republic of the Rio Grande. The Texans established commercial relations with the fractious republic while maintaining an officially neutral posture, partly because they still hoped to negotiate peace with Mexico and partly because they had not ruled out the possibility of one day acquiring Mexico's northern territories for themselves. By 1841, with the collapse of James Treat's peace efforts, the Texans despaired of gaining Mexican recognition and explored a more belligerent policy. Under President Lamar, Texas contracted with federalist rebels in Yucatán—a state remote from central Mexico where secessionist sentiment was strong—to supply three ships from the Texas navy to patrol the sea lanes between Yucatán and Veracruz. Many Texans hoped that an alliance with Yucatán might blossom into a wider war, but Sam Houston, elected to his second term at the end of 1841, ordered the fleet to return.

President Lamar, far more belligerent than Sam Houston, never abandoned the hope of relieving Mexico of more of its territory. Lamar was aware that the trade between Missouri and the Mexican territory of New Mexico was worth some $5 million per year. He therefore hatched a scheme ostensibly aimed at redirecting some portion of that trade toward Texas. Acting without the approval of congress, he assembled a force of 265 soldiers and merchants and sent them forth in June 1841 with seventy head of cattle and several ox-drawn wagons loaded with about $200,000 in merchandise. The expedition was told to remain peaceful unless the authorities at Santa Fe tried to prevent their dealing with the people. Having heard that "revolutionary spirit [was] warm in New Mexico," Lamar clearly hoped the expedition would inspire the New Mexicans to follow the example of Texas. If all went extremely well, it was just possible that an independent New Mexico might end up annexed to the Republic of Texas. The party traveled some thirteen hundred miles over beautiful but harsh terrain, suffering Indian attacks and food shortages that forced them to subsist on lizards and weeds. A small Mexican detachment intercepted them at the outskirts of Santa Fe and compelled them to surrender. The Texans were then forced to march two thousand miles to central Mexico, where they were confined for several months in dreadful prisons.

The Mexicans, too, engaged in periodic belligerence. In March 1842 fourteen hundred Mexican troops under General Rafael Vásquez managed to take the city of San Antonio and the towns of Goliad and Refugio without a fight. Apparently intended as a merely symbolic maneuver, Vásquez's forces withdrew a few days later without doing any damage. Sam Houston, just then starting his second stint as Texas president with a bare treasury and hopelessly stagnant economy, tried mightily to dampen the Texans' growing war fever. He vetoed a bill passed by congress granting him emergency powers and declaring offensive war against Mexico, facing down the resulting outrage, which included open threats of assassination.

In September, Mexican troops once again took San Antonio, but Texas troops managed to chase the Mexicans southward and forced them to retreat across the Rio Grande. The troops pursuing the Mexicans were ordered to stand down at the border, but one group of three hundred men defied that order. They crossed over into Mexico, encountering and unwisely engaging a force of some 2,000 Mexican troops at the riverside village of Mier. Soundly defeated and forced to surrender, 226 survivors were then marched southward. Some of the prisoners managed to escape en route, but they got lost in the mountains of northern Mexico. Several starved to death, and the rest were recaptured. Santa Anna ordered that the entire group be executed, but his generals at the scene opted instead for a gruesome lottery wherein every tenth man was shot. The rest were held at various prisons in central Mexico till late summer of 1844. As in the aftermath of the Alamo and Goliad, the harsh treatment meted out to Texan prisoners provoked much thumping of the war drums, which caused further problems for the beleaguered Sam Houston.

Texas's relations with the United States were not much better than its relations with Mexico. In 1843 Sam Houston launched a fairly risky gambit that led to a minor crisis with the United States. Texas, always inclined to overestimate its own size, claimed that its northernmost boundary reached the Arkansas River, well into the modern state of Kansas. Both Mexican and American caravans plying the Santa Fe Trail from Missouri to New Mexico routinely traversed this area. The Texans indignantly denounced such commerce as "illicit and contraband," vowing to put a stop to it—something that might have the dual benefits of harming Mexican commerce while bringing additional customs revenues into the Texas treasury. Some Texans interpreted this threat to mean that Mexican merchants were fair game for violent attack, and a few hapless Mexicans fell prey to Texan marauders. U.S. authorities, hopeful of protecting their own merchants and eager to refute Mexican charges that they were in cahoots with the Texans, did their best to suppress such doings by providing military escorts to both American and Mexican merchants.

Houston's government commissioned an expedition of about a hundred men under the command of Colonel Jacob Snively to venture north with orders to intercept traders and force them to pay Texas tariffs. Shortly after reaching the Arkansas River, Snively's forces encountered a detachment of U.S. soldiers detailed to guard a caravan of U.S. merchants. To Snively's great surprise and indignation, the U.S. forces detained and disarmed the Texans. The Americans charged that the Texans were planning to menace the caravan under their protection and that the Texans had illegally invaded U.S. territory. The Texas government howled its protests, insisting that the U.S. commander's conduct more closely resembled "the perfidy and cruelty of a savage than . . . the honor, fidelity, and magnanimity which was to be expected from one holding the high rank of an American officer." The dispute was smoothed over soon enough, but it brought no benefit to Texas.

Despite occasional bouts of bellicosity like the Snively expedition, Sam Houston remained devoted to the idea of negotiating an armistice formally ending hostilities with Mexico. He thereby earned the wrath of certain irascible Texans who, when not fighting one another in violent land disputes, tended to vent their wrath on Houston, periodically burning him in effigy. While ensconced in delicate armistice negotiations, Houston was embarrassed when his top naval officer, Commodore Edwin Moore, entered into a plainly illegal scheme to aid federalist rebels in Yucatán. Houston made the unpopular decision to prosecute Moore, and the denunciations of the belligerent Texans predictably grew still more heated.

There were also some very promising developments. On June 13, 1843, Houston proclaimed a unilateral armistice with Mexico; Santa Anna responded by ordering his troops at the border to cease all hostilities. Santa Anna seemed to be moving toward a more conciliatory posture toward Texas, and in this he received strong, constant encouragement—though few solid commitments—from England and France, which were anxious to shepherd through a rapprochement between Mexico and Texas in hopes that Texas might become a bulwark against further U.S. expansion. But before anything could come of this effort, all three countries—Texas, Mexico, and the United States—underwent changes of leadership. The new leaders quickly put an end to all hopes for a happy outcome.

THE THREE-HOUR REVOLUTION

In early 1845 Santa Anna's political career appeared once again to come crashing to an end. Since his election as president in November 1843, he had been writing a fresh and highly creative chapter in the history of bad government.

Santa Anna was not on hand for his electoral triumph in November 1843, having predictably retired to his Veracruz estate a month earlier. General Valentín Canalizo served as acting president, though it was clear that he merely followed Santa Anna's dictates. The Mexican elite had wanted Busta-mante ousted largely because he sought to burden them with taxes, and they apparently thought Santa Anna would treat them more kindly. They thought wrong.

Santa Anna did not exaggerate the government's desperate need for funds. It needed money to service debts owed to the United States, and as usual it needed money for the army. The northern state of Sonora was in a state of virtual civil war, which the central government was unable to suppress. Puebla and Oaxaca had revolted against centralism, while Yu-catán attained near-total autonomy by the end of 1843. The dream of reconquering Texas remained the holy grail for Mexican politicians, especially for Santa Anna. In fact, how-ever, there was little hope that the Mexican army would prevail against the Texans. The War Ministry estimated its annual needs at 22 million pesos, which was nearly twice the treasury's expected yearly revenues.

The unlikelihood of triumph did not dampen the ardor with which Santa Anna sought funds. He coerced loans from the hombres de bien, seizing and auctioning off the goods of those who resisted. He insisted he had the right to ap-point officers of the Catholic Church, and he preyed on the church's wealth through forced loans and confiscations. He slashed the salaries of public employees and raised taxes nearly across the board. He irritated foreigners by raising im-port duties, closing foreign-owned shops, and publishing a list of prohibited imports, which included such unusual items as dog collars and cigar boxes. And of course he persecuted opponents and stifled the press.

To make matters worse, even while taxes and confiscations grew steadily more burdensome, Santa Anna's personal fortune waxed impressively. He added new properties in Veracruz to his already-substantial empire, swelling his full-time workforce to around five thousand. He spent vast amounts of time and money at the cockfights and gaming tables, and he was a regular at lavish banquets and dances, barely bothering to disguise his venality and excess. What was more, although taxes were rising drastically, virtually no progress was being made on the projects that supposedly justified those tax increases: states remained in rebellion; Texas remained independent; debts and salaries remained unpaid.

As his popularity slumped, Santa Anna, the inveterate gambler, apparently counted on divine intervention. In the past, it seemed that whenever his fortunes ebbed, some dramatic crisis would come along, allowing him to play the hero and shore up his base anew. In 1829 it had been the Spanish invasion; in 1838 it was his heroism against the French. Timely exhibitions of reckless courage were capable of distracting the Mexican people from a host of domestic woes. In May 1844 he apparently got his wish: a messenger arrived at Santa Anna's country estate with the tidings that President John Tyler of the United States had submitted to Congress a treaty annexing Texas. This was sensational news indeed, for in August of the previous year Santa Anna's foreign minister had rashly told the U.S. ambassador to Mexico that if the United States annexed Texas, Mexico would deem this "sufficient for the immediate proclamation of war."[5]

The course was clear: Santa Anna would now stake his political career on an attempt to rally the people of Mexico for a grand campaign to subdue the Texans once and for all. He asked congress to approve a four-million-peso appropriation for this purpose, though he did not specify where the money was to come from. The government commanded state governors to furnish troops, but it provided no funds to make such a task possible. All able-bodied men between eighteen and thirty years of age were declared eligible for conscription, though the rich could hire substitutes. According to the British ambassador in Mexico City, hapless "recruits (chained together) are arriving daily."[6]

This time Santa Anna's grandstanding failed to save his fading reputation. Politicians had been milking the cash cow of a chimerical Texas campaign for years, so Santa Anna's blustering was met with cold cynicism. The outfitting of the troops for the hypothetical campaign featured appalling and undisguised graft. Santa Anna won some momentary sympathy when, on August 23, his much-respected wife of nineteen years died after an illness of several weeks. But then, a mere five weeks after his wife's funeral, he had the poor taste to announce his engagement to María Dolores Tosta, a girl of fifteen (Santa Anna was fifty). The general reaction was one of stunned disgust.

As the situation grew more desperate, congress grew restive and by October was in something close to full revolt. Legislators demanded to know what was being done with the extra taxes that were being collected and why the salaries of civil servants continued to go unpaid. In November General Mariano Paredes y Arrillaga rose up in arms. He denounced Santa Anna's taxes and his many abuses of power and demanded that he be ejected from office and made to account for some 60 million pesos spent over the preceding two years. At the same time another large armed peasant rebellion erupted in the southern state of Guerrero, providing an additional irritation for the increasingly besieged dictator.

The newly betrothed Santa Anna returned to the capital in November and quickly left with an army of eleven thousand men to suppress the Paredes revolt. Santa Anna gave Vice President Valentín Canalizo a remarkable set of instructions: he was to silence the opposition press, disband congress, restore order, and raise funds for the Texas campaign without increasing taxes.

Canalizo did his best to carry out Santa Anna's orders. On December 1, while the congress was taking a brief recess from its regular meeting, Canalizo had the doors to the congressional chambers locked and placed under armed guard, charging that the congressmen were subverting the war against Texas. Unfortunately for Santa Anna and Canalizo, this time no one seemed to take their despotism very seriously. The press continued its denunciations, congress refused to disband, and such notables as the Supreme Court justices, the archbishop of Mexico, and Mexico City's municipal council all issued formal protests against the closure of congress. On December 5 another rebellion erupted in the capital itself, this one led by General José Joaquín de Herrera, president of Santa Anna's own Council of Government.

The congressmen met with Herrera at a monastery around noon on December 6, from whence they sent a note to Canalizo demanding that the constitutional order be restored. By this time Canalizo had evidently lost all support, including that of the army. He agreed to the congressmen's demands on the condition that his safety and that of his ministers be guaranteed. Herrera agreed to this demand by three p.m., and with that the Three Hour Revolution was all over except the celebrating.

But what a celebration it was! The congressmen made a symbolic march from the monastery to the congressional chamber. As they went forth, they were hailed as heroes. Church bells tolled joyously, while cheering crowds, armed with clubs, swords, rifles, and many makeshift weapons, surged through the streets bearing some of the congressmen on their shoulders. Some members of the enthusiastic mob busied themselves with the task of demolishing the monuments that Santa Anna had intended as his own heroic legacy.

One group broke into the Santa Anna Theatre and demolished a plaster statue of the dictator. Others toppled and destroyed the bronze statue of Santa Anna in the Plaza del Volador, and all over the city portraits of the dictator were defaced. The supreme indignity came when crowds entered the Santa Paula cemetery, disinterred Santa Anna's amputated leg (which had been buried with such solemn ceremony a little over two years before), tied it to a rope, and dragged it gleefully through the streets crying "Death to the Cripple, Long Live Congress!" Volunteer militias rallied enthusiastically, and in early January Santa Anna was decisively defeated at Puebla, his forces scattered. He was arrested and sentenced to a life in exile at half a general's pay. He left Mexico on June 3, 1845.

The Revolution of 1844 was undeniably a cathartic moment. Soon came the inevitable comparisons to England's Glorious Revolution of 1688, for this was nothing less than a truly popular revolution against an abusive and tyrannical government, accomplished entirely without bloodshed. Messages of support poured in from all corners of the republic, and Mexicans permitted themselves a rare moment of optimism. Unfortunately, it soon became clear that the revolution was illusory. Federalism and liberalism appeared triumphant for the moment, but conservatives and centralists bided their time, plotting a comeback. Personal and political antagonisms remained as strong as ever. The reconquest of Texas, elusive though it was, remained a staple in feverish political rants. Most ominous of all, the looming prospect of U.S. annexation of Texas and possible war created an atmosphere of crisis, which was hardly conducive to sound decision-making. Instead of entering upon a new era of popular government, Mexico embarked on one of the most tumultuous times in its history.

6

THE ANNEXATION CRISIS

The idea that the United States should annex Texas was certainly not new in 1844, but in that year it seemed suddenly to gain a ferocious momentum that affected several nations and many competing interests. Texas annexation would likely have proved divisive no matter how it was accomplished, but the fact that it was accomplished by ethically and legally dubious means ensured that it would provoke crises and that those crises would be severe. The political crisis it provoked within the United States became an important cause of the Civil War of the 1860s. Annexation also provoked yet another round of severe political crises in Mexico, as well as a series of attempted interventions by European powers anxious to halt the territorial expansion of the United States.

THE ANNEXATION DEBATE
IN THE UNITED STATES

In the United States sentiment was badly split on the issue of territorial expansion in general and on the acquisition of

Texas in particular. Critics of expansion held that the wealth and cares brought by expansion would doom democracy, just as it had done in ancient Athens and republican Rome. Others suspected that expansion was a scheme by southern slave owners to add new slave states and thus increase their power. Proponents of expansion worked hard to overcome such objections, coming up at times with ingenious arguments designed to appease critics while simultaneously increasing the ardor of their fellow expansionists.

No one was more ingenious in devising ways to batter down objections to annexation than Senator Robert J. Walker of Mississippi. A transplanted Pennsylvania lawyer, Walker was well versed in the arguments for and against annexation, and he set about to find the common ground—or rather, to find and exploit useful prejudices common to nearly all white Americans. Northern opponents of slavery may have deplored the "peculiar institution" and wished to see its demise, but that did not mean that they were comfortable with the prospect of living side by side with free blacks on terms of equality. Most, in fact, assumed that the white race would be gravely threatened by emancipation, particularly if it were accomplished precipitately. Walker played cleverly on those racial anxieties.

In 1844 Walker wrote a twenty-six-page letter that was subsequently printed in full in some of the country's leading newspapers and circulated by the millions of copies in pamphlet form. The real threat, Walker explained, was not slavery but the presence of blacks throughout the country. Walker made much use of data from the 1840 census, which were remarkable indeed. The census appeared to give resounding support to the slave owners' long-held contention that slavery was good for blacks, saving them from their own bestial natures and forcing upon them at least the bare rudiments of civilization. Free blacks, the census seemed to show, were *eleven times* more likely to be physically deformed or mentally deranged than slaves. Some pointed out that the census data were implausible, to say the least. In Worcester, Massachusetts, for instance, a whopping 133 out of 151 black residents were classed as insane, and some towns that had no black residents at all appeared in the census as home to shocking numbers of black beggars, cripples, and lunatics. The patent inaccuracy of the data, however, mattered little, for white Americans of the 1840s were generally predisposed to believe the worst about blacks.

They were also generally inclined to think the worst about England, another favorite bugbear. Perhaps Walker's most impressive gambit was to wed anglophobia to negrophobia to advance the annexationist cause. England, according to his reasoning, was intent on mediating the dispute between Mexico and Texas in the hope of persuading Mexico to recognize Texas's independence. That independence would be guaranteed by England on the condition that the Texans agreed neither to seek nor accept annexation to the United States. England would then pressure Texas to abolish slavery, and horrifying consequences would soon follow. Walker and other apologists for slavery were cynical about England's motives, for England had freed the slaves in its West Indian colonies in 1833 and as a result had taken a beating in the colonial sugar trade. Accordingly, Walker charged, the British hoped to push abolition elsewhere, not for altruistic reasons but so that its West Indian products would become more competitive. Moreover, England would set up preferential trade with Texas, importing Texas cotton duty free and selling manufactured goods unburdened by the discriminatory tariff charged by the United States. Other states in the U.S. South and Southwest might be tempted to leave the Union and join with Texas so as to gain preferential access to the British market; or the United States might be pressured to end its own protective tariffs, which would damage the U.S. economy and destroy its revenues. In addition to economic concerns, the

United States had to consider a pro-British Texas a threat to its national security, for in the event of hostilities the United States would find itself bordered by Britain or its allies to both north and south. With Texas a British ally, the Gulf of Mexico and Mississippi River would be imperiled. Walker's allies, such as President Tyler's secretary of state, Abel Upshur, embellished this nightmarish picture by pointing out that England might be tempted to goad American blacks to revolt, subverting U.S. security from within.

In short, the consequences of not annexing Texas, as outlined by Walker, would be alarming: Americans of every section of the country would soon find themselves surrounded by weak-minded, physically deformed, and morally depraved black people; the country would face economic depression, civil war, and dismemberment; and America's most powerful enemy would be handed a potent weapon with which to menace the nation's security. On the other hand, should annexation be accomplished, it would bring untold blessings to all Americans. Those who assumed that annexation would be a boon to the forces of slavery erred, for ultimately the outcome would be precisely the opposite. Surprisingly, Walker argued, annexation would be a first step toward ridding the United States of the baneful institution of slavery. Slaves and their owners would be attracted to the warm climate and other enticements that Texas offered, and more and more of them would migrate southward. Texas would be a gateway to the still more agreeable climes of Mexico and Central and South America. Blacks in those countries would mix with Indians, affording them a step up in the racial hierarchy. In time, all blacks, both enslaved and free, would be drained away from the United States, leaving it an all-white republic—for many whites in 1840s America, a highly desirable outcome. Walker, hoping to allay the widespread suspicion that annexation was part of a conspiracy by southern slave owners, was at pains to point out that southern slave owners were not the only ones who stood to benefit from the acquisition of Texas; nor would they be the biggest losers should annexation fail.

Arguments such as Walker's certainly did not persuade the most adamant opponents of annexation, some of whom gleefully ridiculed the particulars. But the prospect of ending slavery and racial strife so painlessly gave the arguments widespread appeal. According to the Richmond *Enquirer*, they continued for months to be "the theme, the talk, the fashion, the very rage."[1] The specific arguments regarding race and commerce blended nicely with the imperious pronouncements of writers like John L. O'Sullivan, coiner of the phrase "Manifest Destiny," that dismissed such niceties as "rights of discovery, exploration, settlement, contiguity, etc.," as mere quibbling. Providence had simply and unambiguously intended the United States to spread its "great experiment of liberty and federative self government" across the North American continent, and the nation's right to extra territory was as natural and unquestionable "as that of the tree to the space of air and earth suitable for the full expansion of its principle and destiny of growth." Any who complained proved, by the very act of complaining, that they were unworthy of the possession of valuable real estate. "Public sentiment with us," editorialized the *New York Morning News* in 1845, "repudiates possession without use . . . This national policy, necessity or destiny, we know to be just and beneficent, and we can, therefore, afford to scorn the invective and imputations of rival nations."[2] Such arguments made for a heady brew of artless optimism and hubris and they were, for the moment at least, intoxicating enough to overcome divisions over slavery and section.

With the aid of such visionary polemics, sentiment in favor of annexing Texas had been gaining ground steadily since 1841, and by 1844 a large segment of the American public was ready to be persuaded. The arguments had persuaded

President John Tyler, a lanky Virginia planter and slave owner, who had succeeded to the presidency in 1841 upon the death of William Henry Harrison. Earlier in his career Tyler had bolted the Democratic Party for the Whig Party, and his subsequent disputes with the Whigs had led to his expulsion from that party as well. He was thus an unelected president without a party and only a slender base of support. He hoped to ride the issue of Texas annexation to popularity and possibly reelection. But the Whigs, led by Henry Clay, eloquently objected that the addition of Texas would upset the delicate balance of power between North and South and lead inevitably to war with Mexico. The Senate rejected Tyler's treaty of annexation in June 1844, only six months before the end of his term. Tyler dropped out of the presidential race, leaving the struggle to the anti-annexation Whig candidate Henry Clay and his yet-to-be-chosen Democratic Party rival.

There was tension among Democrats on the expansion issue. The early front-runner for the nomination was Martin Van Buren, who shared with Clay the conviction that Tyler's rush to annexation was reckless. Determined proannexationists, including Robert J. Walker, maneuvering deftly at the Democratic convention, managed to persuade their party to repudiate Van Buren and opt instead for a dark horse candidate known to favor annexation, former Tennessee congressman and governor James K. Polk.

The Democratic Party platform under Polk came to advocate the "*re*annexation" of Texas, claiming that Texas had in fact been part of the 1803 Louisiana Purchase, which had been bargained away in the 1819 Adams-Onís treaty with Spain. That tactic had two advantages: it used semantics to make Texas annexation seem a matter of elementary justice, while also taking a swipe at the negotiator of the 1819 treaty, John Quincy Adams, who was currently the most vocal critic of Texas annexation. Adams and his coreligionaries took the view that annexation would be unconstitutional, would risk an unnecessary and dishonorable war, and would worsen the slavery problem. By contrast, Democratic candidate Polk—a small, intense, uncharismatic, and humorless man—refused to acknowledge any connection between territorial expansion and slavery and had no doubts about the moral superiority and special destiny of Anglo-Saxon Americans. After a bitter campaign Polk won the presidency by a scant thirty-eight thousand votes. He and his supporters interpreted this slender victory as nothing less than a "mandate" for Texas annexation.

President Tyler, still hopeful of pushing through Texas annexation on his watch, proposed that Texas be invited into the Union through a joint resolution rather than a treaty. The resolution would be easier to get passed, needing only a simple majority vote in both houses of Congress. According to the resolution, Texas would be immediately offered admission to the Union as a state—presumably one in which slavery would be legal. The amendment passed the House but stalled in the Senate. Senator Walker proposed a solution to the Senate impasse: incoming President Polk would have the option of accepting the resolution as passed by the House or negotiating a new treaty with the Texans. Polk, eager to see the resolution passed as quickly as possible, apparently allowed opponents of the original resolution to believe he preferred negotiating a new treaty with Texas in which slavery might be excluded and the boundary dispute resolved. With that understanding, enough senators switched their votes to allow the amended joint resolution to pass 27–25.

The two-option compromise was evidently nothing but a political ploy. On March 3, his last day in office, President Tyler sent a courier to Texas with an offer of immediate annexation. Polk endorsed Tyler's actions upon entering office. He also pointedly declared that the Rio Grande was to be the nonnegotiable boundary of the U.S. state of Texas. The re-

fusal to negotiate on the disputed territory was clearly a
provocation, one that Polk was prepared to exploit should
diplomacy with Mexico fail.

TEXAS, MEXICO, AND THE
GREAT POWERS OF EUROPE

The American expansionists may have exaggerated in their
denunciations of British intrigues, but those intrigues were
not entirely a matter of paranoid fantasy. England paid close
attention to Texas issues, having good reasons for wanting to
see that republic remain independent and prosperous. England was apprehensive about the growing size and power of
the United States and hoped Texas might prove useful in
stemming that tide. And just as Walker and his allies asserted,
England assumed that an independent cotton-growing Texas
would provide a cheap and reliable source of raw materials for
British factories, as well as a healthy market for the output
of those factories. Also, British merchants and bondholders
hoped that a strong, independent Texas would increase the
chances that Mexico might one day repay its debts, for it
would remove Mexico's pretext for lavishing its scant resources on its bloated army. Finally, the British feared that
Texas annexation to the United States would perpetuate slavery there. An independent Texas beholden to England might
be induced to abolish that evil institution.

Lord Aberdeen, the British foreign secretary, appeared disposed to take strong measures in defense of Texas. Four obstacles, however, stood in the way of success. First, the Texans
themselves seemed eager to join the United States and would
have to be persuaded that independence was a more desirable
option. Second, the Mexicans continued obstinately to refuse
to acknowledge Texas's independence. They would have to be
persuaded that recognition of Texas would bring tangible
benefits without damaging their national dignity. Third, En-

gland would have to proceed somewhat delicately, since it was even then embroiled in an acrimonious dispute with the United States over the Oregon Territory, which both countries claimed. England was not eager for war with the United States. And finally, in order to achieve a happy outcome, England would likely have to enlist the support of France. François Guizot, who wielded executive power in France, was interested in cooperating, but here again there were obstacles. France had blockaded and attacked Mexico as recently as 1838, and her relations with Mexico remained poor. Nor were Anglo-French relations entirely harmonious, despite the personal rapport between Guizot and Aberdeen. The majority of the French people rather liked the idea of Texas annexation to the United States, for no better reason than that the prospect was displeasing to the British. Keeping Texas independent would not be an easy task.

In late May 1844, as the U.S. Senate was close to rejecting President Tyler's annexation treaty, Aberdeen spoke with the diplomatic representatives of both Texas and Mexico, outlining his plan for what he called a "diplomatic act" respecting Texas. According to this plan, if Mexico agreed to recognize Texas's independence, England and France would jointly guarantee that independence, and they would also ensure that Mexico would retain possession of New Mexico and California. If the United States should go ahead with its annexation plans, England and France would "assist Mexico in the contest which may be thereby brought on."[3]

This plan had little chance of success. The French, faced with the possibility of war with the United States, responded tepidly to Aberdeen's suggestions. Meanwhile the British and French ministers at Washington warned that any suggestion of British and French meddling in Texas might doom the candidacy of anti-annexationist Henry Clay, thus playing into the hands of the annexationists. The Texans, for their part, wished to keep their options open. Anson Jones, who won the

Texas presidency in September 1844, openly complained that Texas had been "shabbily used" by the United States, and he generally viewed the Europeans warmly. Outgoing president Sam Houston—who according to one of his critics favored annexation when sober and violently opposed it when drunk—apparently urged acceptance of the British plan. Even so, Jones was skeptical of the idea: the diplomatic act would give England the right to arbitrate American disputes, doom any prospect of annexation, and possibly lead to war between Europe and America. Jones instructed Texas diplomats to cease discussing the plan, and the diplomatic act came to naught.

The Mexicans, for their part, did little to help advance any sort of diplomatic settlement. At the very moment when the British and French were exploring a negotiated settlement of the Mexico-Texas dispute, Santa Anna was escalating his bombast, vowing that the invasion of Texas would begin any day and that all Texas prisoners would be summarily shot as traitors. The British explicitly assured Santa Anna that, should he invade Texas and find himself in difficulties, "he must not look for the support of Great Britain in aiding him to extricate himself from those difficulties." French king Louis Philippe personally harangued the Mexican minister to France on the topic, accusing the Mexicans of "infatuation" with Texas. "This infatuation," he said, "prevents you from recognizing what everybody else sees; that is, that you have lost Texas irrevocably."[4]

The Mexican stance toward recognizing Texas was not entirely unreasonable. The Mexicans argued that it would be folly to trust in the good faith of Texans, who had repeatedly proved themselves unreliable. If Mexico were to recognize Texas as an independent country, what assurance would it have that the Texans would not subsequently seek annexation to the United States? Or that they would refrain from attacking Mexico? Indeed, Mexican recognition would increase these possibilities, since by granting recognition Mexico would be acknowledging that the Texans were free to do whatever they pleased. The Mexicans maintained that the Texans, like all savage peoples, respected only the threat of physical force. If the British and French wanted Mexico to recognize Texas independence, they must agree unequivocally to supply that force. Despite these arguments, Santa Anna eventually softened on the issue. He agreed to recognize Texas in late November 1844 in exchange for a generous indemnity from the United States and a British and French commitment to defend a favorable boundary. But the British and French once again backed away from granting hard and fast guarantees, and Santa Anna's government was overthrown a week later.

The Mexican attitude toward Texas softened even more after Santa Anna's ouster. The dictator's successor, General José Joaquín de Herrera, was a dedicated moderate. He was, like Santa Anna, a native of Veracruz state, and like Santa Anna he had joined the Spanish royal army while still a teenager. Except for a brief stint as a druggist, he had spent his entire career in the army. But unlike Santa Anna, Herrera sought sincerely to reconcile Mexico's irreconcilable factions while scrupulously avoiding rash acts. Although of modest financial means himself, he was comfortable in the company of the hombres de bien, and he shared their uneasiness toward the commoners. In a refreshing contrast to so many others, he was known for his honesty and integrity, common sense and sound judgment, though in some ways his modesty and moderation made him poorly suited to times of crisis: when so many demanded heroics, Herrera offered only sober, unglamorous reason. Nor did he possess the kind of dynamic personality that might have helped him sell his policies effectively.

Herrera, of course, confronted the same problems that had already undone so many previous regimes. Mexico's total revenues amounted to less than half of expenses. The single largest expense remained the army, which continued to claim budget priority by conjuring the Texas menace. Factionalism, too, remained a volatile problem. The constitution Herrera inherited from the Santa Anna dictatorship, the so-called Organic Bases, was wildly unpopular, and it provided the radical liberals—who began styling themselves *puros*, to distinguish themselves from the *moderados*, or moderate federalists—with a potent issue. The constitution restricted citizenship to people of means, concentrated power in Mexico City, reduced the states to "departments," and allowed for no civil rights. But while puros demanded an immediate resurrection of the federalist Constitution of 1824, Herrera merely appointed a committee to consider constitutional reform. Such dallying cost him a great deal of political support.

By far the most heated rhetoric, however, swirled around the perennial hot-button issue of Texas. Herrera was well aware that Mexico was in no condition to risk war with the United States. Moreover, he had seen how Santa Anna's efforts to rally the nation for an invasion of Texas had fizzled. Herrera, in fact, was strongly inclined to avert war by recognizing Texas independence, with Mexico availing itself of whatever good offices Britain and France might be willing to provide. He managed to get authorization from congress to open negotiations with Texas, and he had strong support in his quest for an "honorable treaty" from moderates. The more radical puros, however, lost no opportunity to make political hay out of Herrera's alleged weakness and cowardice.

While much of what the politicians and journalists wrote and said was simply irresponsible demagoguery, they did make some points that were not easily gainsaid. Mexicans who followed the debates on annexation that raged in U.S. newspapers were alarmed by the blatantly racist rhetoric they found there. Anglo-Saxon Americans clearly considered Mexicans their racial inferiors, lumping them into the same category as blacks and Indians. Given that the Americans had enslaved blacks and exterminated or relocated Indians, Mexicans could not be sanguine about what fate might befall them should the Americans conquer their country. Mexicans were also well aware of the inflammatory rhetoric of racial destiny that was reaching a crescendo in the 1840s. While some U.S. writers claimed that the destiny of Anglo-Saxons was to uplift and civilize benighted peoples, others argued that it was simply to overwhelm and displace those peoples who held valuable resources undeservingly. "When the white races of this country multiply as they will multiply to a certain extent," wrote James Gordon Bennett of the influential *New York Herald* in 1844, "all the colored races will disappear. We have seen that problem already solved and determined in the case of the Indian races."[5] The Americans appeared to have nothing but disdain for the way the Mexicans had been utilizing their lands. Were they, too, destined to "disappear"? And who could say when the Americans would be satisfied with the extent of their territory? Resistance might indeed be futile, some maintained, but the question was one of national survival. Mexicans simply had no choice but to fight.

While these concerns may have had merit, puro politicians flogged them to the point of hysteria. To judge from the tone of some liberal newspapers and broadsides, one would have thought that war fever was sweeping Mexico. "Federation and war on Texas," declared *La Voz del Pueblo*, "that is the cry of the people."[6] Former vice president Valentín Gómez Farías, who had spent much time in exile, returned to Mexico in March 1845 and assumed leadership of the radical faction, becoming the most strident advocate of war against Texas. Gómez Farías maintained that the reconquest of Texas was absolutely indispensable to Mexico's prosperity, and he even suggested that it would be a fairly easy undertaking: the Texans, he claimed, were badly divided, and the largely Mexican population of San Antonio would support Mexico against the Texans. The campaign should begin at once.

Such was the situation in Mexico when James K. Polk was elected president of the United States—an event that British newspapers denounced as "the triumph of everything that is worst" in America—and the annexation resolution was passed. The Mexican minister to Washington Juan N. Almonte, in accordance with his instructions, immediately requested his passports, severed diplomatic relations between the United States and Mexico, and returned home to help Mexico prepare for war.

Despite Almonte's precipitous action, all was not necessarily lost. The annexation resolution still needed the approval of the Texans, and that they would grant it was not an entirely foregone conclusion. Both Sam Houston and his successor, Anson Jones, had well-known doubts about the matter. They, like many Texans, had assumed that Texas would be welcomed into the Union immediately after winning its independence, and they were offended by the long delay. Their most cherished hope was that the United States might offer annexation at the same time Mexico offered recognition, so that Texans could make a reasoned decision between independence and statehood. Jones pointedly avoided the annexation issue during his campaign, made no mention of it in his inaugural address, and continued his silence even after the resolution was approved in the U.S. Congress. The British and French representatives urged him to delay action for ninety days, simultaneously lending their good offices to help Texas obtain recognition from Mexico. By this time Britain and France had abandoned any notion of giving Mexico any solid guarantees, especially ones involving the use of force. They were resolved only to use their "moral influence" to bring the Mexicans around.

Diplomacy finally bore fruit. On May 19, 1845, Mexico agreed to formally recognize the independence of Texas on the condition that Texas agree not be annexed to the United States. Boundary issues were to be resolved later through negotiation and arbitration. Anson Jones got his wish and was now able to present his fellow Texans with a choice between annexation and independence.

As it turned out, the reservations that Houston and Jones had toward annexation were not widely shared by their fellow Texans. The U.S. chargé d'affaires to Texas, Andrew Jackson Donelson, nephew of Old Hickory and a skilled diplomat in his own right, had spent months in Texas ardently promoting annexation. The Texas congress had already come out strongly for annexation. The vast majority of Texans favored annexation and zealously resented Jones's tepidness on the matter, to the point of burning him in effigy and threatening him with ouster. Upon receiving the news of Mexican willingness to recognize Texas's independence, Jones called a convention to consider the two offers. Meeting at Austin on July 4, the convention wasted little time before rejecting Mexico's offer of recognition and accepting annexation by a lopsided vote of fifty-five to one. After taking care of the remaining details, Jones was able to declare on February 19, 1846, that "the final act in this great drama is now performed; the Republic of Texas is no more."

THE FAILURE OF DIPLOMACY

The news that Texas had accepted annexation to the United States was a tremendous blow to Herrera and his moderate allies. Stung by the failure of his conciliatory policy and a barrage of abuse from his domestic critics, Herrera was virtually forced to rattle some sabers, declaring that Mexico would fight to defend her honor. After all, Mexico had declared publicly that it would view annexation as an act of war.

The Polk administration missed few chances to fan the flames of Mexico's war hysteria. It clung fiercely to its contention that Texas was bounded to the south by the Rio

Grande, not the Nueces as it had been when it was a Mexican state. Polk ordered General Zachary Taylor, the commander at Fort Jesup in western Louisiana, to move his troops toward the Rio Grande. By mid-July Taylor's forces were encamped at Corpus Christi, just inside the disputed territory. Meanwhile, papers allied to the Polk administration were denouncing the "insolence, stupidity and folly" of the Mexicans, ridiculing their threats of war. Apparently Polk and his supporters believed that bellicosity was the best way to bring the Mexicans to the bargaining table. In fact, bellicosity had precisely the opposite effect: it inspired fear, humiliation, and rage, playing squarely into the hands of Mexico's war party. Herrera, with few options, sent Mexican troops to the Rio Grande with orders to remain south of the river and to avoid hostilities.

The Mexican army was in no sense prepared for war with the United States. "Strictly speaking," lamented one moderate Mexican politician, "the army does not exist. What today bears that name is only a mass of men without training and without weapons."[7] Mexican officers might create an impressive spectacle with their fine mounts and gaudy uniforms, but many were political hacks whose loyalty was questionable and who lacked the most basic military competence. According to one estimate, there were eighteen officers for every five regular soldiers, and those officers' bloated salaries were ruinous to the budget. Service in the Mexican army was infamously unattractive, so recruits had to be coerced. Prisoners, vagrants, and drunkards were pressed into service. Indians were often captured, quite literally, with lassos as they tried to flee from recruiters, and brought to the barracks chained together. Discipline was notoriously derelict. Brantz Mayer, secretary of the U.S. legation during the 1840s, recounted seeing a sergeant at Veracruz drilling a few recruits "to the tap of the drum. The music seemed to be a dead march, and the step of the soldiers was slow and solemn. Nothing could be more dreary—more heart-sickening."[8] Armaments were scarce and of low quality. Mexico had no firearms factories, so most of the army's weapons were antiquated muskets purchased at bargain prices in Europe, which were useless except at short range. U.S. minister to Mexico Waddy Thompson guessed that no more than one in ten recruits had ever seen a gun prior to doing service, and fewer than one in a hundred had actually fired one. Food and clothing were likewise scarce. Under such circumstances desertion was an entirely sensible option and was often employed. In 1845 General Mariano Arista, who commanded the Mexican forces at the northern frontier, complained that of the four thousand troops who had been sent to the border since 1841, all had deserted, and he was left with only a small corps of veterans on the very eve of hostilities with the United States.

To his credit, Herrera did try to reform the military. He simplified the command structure, changed the system of promotions to reward merit rather than partisan allegiance, and clearly delineated the powers of state governors and military officers in hopes of eliminating the problem of regional caudillos. Most controversially, he tried to revive the idea of a civic militia—an idea that had fallen on hard times during the era of centralized government. He authorized the creation of a new force to be known as the Volunteers in Defense of Independence and the Law, which was supposed to serve as a counterweight to the regular army and, to some extent, give Mexicans a greater stake in their own defense. Unfortunately, Herrera handled the matter clumsily. Many who might have served in such a force were incensed that Herrera had disbanded the volunteer militias that had formed spontaneously to defeat Santa Anna in January 1845. It was presumed that Herrera feared that those militias might turn against his own government, lending considerable credence to the charge that Herrera simply did not trust the common folk. The charge was further borne out by the details of Herrera's proposal:

service in the new militia was to be voluntary and unpaid, and the prerequisites for service—militiamen had to have incomes of at least two hundred pesos per year and could not be artisans or public servants—excluded all but wealthy Mexicans. Recruitment was disappointing, to say the least. The largest unit was in Morelia, Michoacán, where a mere thirty-seven volunteers turned out. In many cities, no one volunteered at all. Herrera's failed effort to create a militia turned out to be one of the great disasters of his presidency. It alienated reactionary officers of the regular army and failed to provide for a force that might have risen to defend Herrera's government when it came under attack. Moreover, it did nothing to enhance Mexico's preparedness for war. The Mexican military continued to be manned by unwilling conscripts rather than by patriotic citizens.

Knowing full well that Mexico was in no condition to fight the United States, Herrera sought to explore all options for avoiding war. Unfortunately, peace was an entirely sensible but politically ruinous proposition. Politicians were split into four factions: moderate federalists, who wanted some liberal reforms but shared the elite's horror of the lower classes; radical federalists, who relied on lower-class support and wished to weaken the power of the church and army; traditional conservatives, who were increasingly convinced that only a legitimate European monarch could save the country; and *santanistas*, who believed that only Santa Anna could save the country. Of these factions, only moderate federalists like Herrera consistently advocated a negotiated settlement of the dispute with the United States. Politicians of the three other factions mercilessly attacked Herrera with charges of cowardice.

Herrera did get congress to authorize the raising of a 15-million-peso loan, and there was some discussion of just how to tap into the church's wealth to support a war effort. But Herrera still seemed resolved to continue to work through diplomatic channels as far as possible. He let it be known that he would be willing to discuss the Texas boundary issue if the United States were willing to pay an indemnity. William Parrott, a confidential agent sent by the Polk administration to explore diplomatic options in Mexico, reported that although calls for war were shrill and insistent, the Mexicans' awareness of their own weakness probably meant that an amicable arrangement could be reached. He suggested that the United States send a suitably qualified envoy, predicting that such a person could likely settle all issues "over a breakfast." Taking that advice to heart, Polk selected John Slidell, a generally well-regarded Louisiana politician who spoke Spanish fluently.

For a brief while, prospects for a settlement seemed favorable. U.S. diplomats reported optimistically that Herrera's government might even be persuaded to sell New Mexico and California in addition to Texas. Slidell, accordingly, was authorized to treat for as much territory as he could talk the Mexicans out of. His instructions mentioned the over $3 million in American claims against Mexico, proposing that those claims be liquidated if Mexico agreed to a general boundary adjustment. The instructions forcefully asserted that the Rio Grande was the nonnegotiable southern border of Texas, and that the United States was prepared to pay $5 million in exchange for Texas and New Mexico. The payment would rise to as much as $25 million if Mexico would toss in California, including San Francisco and Monterey with their valuable harbors. Privately, Polk assured Slidell that if the Mexicans proved recalcitrant, he was prepared to make an issue of U.S. claims against Mexico, taking "redress for the wrongs and injuries we have suffered."

Slidell arrived in Mexico City on December 6, 1845, and was greeted by a tempest of angry diatribes in the Mexican press denouncing the Americans and accusing Herrera of plotting to sell Mexico's northern territories. Some editorials openly advocated overthrowing the Herrera government "before it is too late." Herrera, shocked by the vehemence of the denunciations, quickly determined that it would be a mistake to receive Slidell. The U.S. government had in fact provided the Mexicans with a convenient pretext for refusing to receive him: Slidell carried the title "minister plenipotentiary" to Mexico. Mexico had agreed to receive only a "commissioner." To receive a minister would imply that Mexico had resumed full diplomatic relations with the United States, something Herrera insisted only congress was empowered to do and that in any case would likely be done only if the United States expressed sufficient contrition to permit Mexico to resume relations in a face-saving way.

Herrera's last-minute change of heart made little difference. By the time Slidell arrived in Mexico, the plotting of Herrera's overthrow was already well advanced. The key figure in the plot was the archconservative General Mariano Paredes y Arrillaga, the army commander at San Luis Potosí who had helped bring Herrera to power the year before. Paredes had for some time been corresponding with Herrera's opponents, including many liberals. Paredes's own sympathies were revealed in his correspondence with the conservative intellectual Lucas Alamán and with the Spanish minister to Mexico Salvador Bermúdez de Castro, who assured Paredes that they could come up with funding to bring a European prince to assume the throne of Mexico. Paredes's loathing of the common folk was extreme even by the standards of the Mexican elite, and like most conservatives he believed that the two pillars of the old colonial order—king and church—were the best means of keeping the poor in their place.

Early in December, when Herrera ordered Paredes to reinforce Mariano Arista's forces in the north, Paredes refused, instead demanding that Herrera resign the presidency. The formal rebellion began on December 14 with the Plan of San

Luis Potosí, which charged Herrera with trying to bargain away precious national territory, creating a militia of the rabble, trying to abolish the army, and generally causing chaos and anarchy. Most army garrisons seconded the revolt. Herrera's government made a show of defiance: speakers in congress called Paredes a scoundrel, a traitor, and a drunkard, and at the last possible moment the government hastily distributed some seven thousand muskets. But Herrera's impromptu militia was easily disarmed, and by the end of December, when the capital garrison joined the revolt, the Herrera government collapsed so unceremoniously that, according to one observer, "any foreigner coming into Mexico would not have the slightest idea that the country had gone through an upheaval."[9]

The hombres de bien were delighted by the Paredes revolt, but most Mexicans were less pleased. Monarchy was not a popular option in Mexico, and Paredes was attacked for his monarchist sympathies and his authoritarian bent. Easily the most ironic of the many charges leveled against Paredes, however, was that he was insufficiently jingoist. He had justified his overthrow of Herrera partly on the grounds that Herrera had no stomach for war, but once in office Paredes proved to be just as anxious to avoid conflict with the United States. John Slidell was guardedly optimistic that the Paredes government would receive him eventually. In late January Slidell left Mexico City for Jalapa, Veracruz, but not before dropping a few hints that he held the answer to Mexico's extreme financial distress.

A patient policy might have borne fruit, but the Americans opted instead to force the issue. President Polk and his secretary of state, James Buchanan, instructed Slidell to continue trying to meet with the government, but at the same time they hinted that if the Mexicans continued to refuse, dire consequences would follow. To reinforce that threat, the administration sent orders to General Taylor, who had been biding his time at Corpus Christi, to move his forces to the Rio Grande and occupy positions at Laredo and Point Isabel, at the river's mouth. At the same time naval squadrons took up stations off Veracruz and Mazatlán. Upon learning of these maneuvers, Slidell grew emboldened: on March 1 he sent an ultimatum to the Mexican foreign minister. Mexico, it said, had two weeks to choose between peace and war.

Once again the apparent assumption that the Mexicans would back down in the face of threats revealed appalling ignorance of the political dynamics within Mexico. Threats and attempts at intimidation were practically guaranteed to offend the Mexicans' sense of honor and incline them toward greater obstinacy. That, in fact, is precisely what Slidell's note accomplished. Paredes's foreign minister, Joaquín Castillo y Lanzas, answered Slidell's brusque note with an equally brusque one. Castillo y Lanzas insisted that the recent military maneuvers in Texas and the Gulf were proof of American bad faith. He accused the United States of having masterminded an elaborate plot to seize Texas and charged that the designation of Slidell as "minister plenipotentiary" was not an oversight but a calculated insult. Slidell, the note made clear, would not be received, and if hostilities should erupt, they would be the fault of the United States. Slidell downplayed the American military presence, refuted the account of the Texas issue, and accused the Mexicans of answering good faith offers of peace with bullheadedness and insults. He prepared to abandon his mission and return home.

Even as Slidell was packing his bags, General Zachary Taylor and his troops were arriving at the banks of the Rio Grande, deep within the disputed territory. General Pedro Ampudia demanded that Taylor move his forces back across the Nueces River within twenty-four hours. Taylor refused; his primary intention was clearly to provoke an incident that would serve as a pretext for war. President Polk made no secret of his conviction that diplomacy had been exhausted and that he was now resolved to declare war: he needed only some plausible pretext. He pondered basing a war declaration on the supposed insult to Slidell, or perhaps on Mexico's failure to pay its debts, but neither option would be ideal. He fervently hoped the Mexicans would attack Taylor's forces in the disputed territory.

On May 8 he got his wish. On that date Zachary Taylor's dispatch arrived at the White House bearing the news that a force of several hundred Mexicans had attacked a small reconnaissance party on April 25 at a place on the Rio Grande about fifteen miles upstream from the present-day site of Brownsville, Texas. Sixteen Americans had been killed or wounded in the melee, the rest taken prisoner. Polk immediately set to work on his war message, which unequivocally branded the Mexicans as the aggressors and the Americans as long-suffering victims:

> The cup of forbearance had been exhausted even before the recent information from the frontier of the Del Norte [Rio Grande]. But now, after reiterated menaces, Mexico has passed the boundary of the United States, has invaded our territory and shed American blood on American soil. She has proclaimed that hostilities have commenced, and that the two nations are now at war.

The declaration was, of course, founded upon a deliberate deception. The Mexicans had not invaded American territory. The Americans, rather, had provoked an attack in territory they claimed on dubious grounds. Polk's maneuvering leaves little room to doubt that he was resolved to relieve Mexico of its northern lands by fair means or foul.

Two battles—Palo Alto and Resaca de la Palma, both victories for the United States—were fought even before the of-

ficial U.S. declaration of war was signed on May 13, and the
call went out for volunteers to help deliver to Mexico her just
punishment. The long-anticipated war between the United
States and Mexico was finally under way.

"Ho," said the most famous recruiting poster, "for the halls
of the Montezumas!"

7

THE WAR OF 1847

As war began, most realistic Mexicans realized that their country had little hope of victory. They thought, however, that they might manage to avoid a crushing defeat. If they could hold the line at the frontier, it would force the United States to launch a risky amphibious invasion. Perhaps the Mexicans could then bottle up the invaders at the coast, where tropical diseases would take a fearsome toll. If all else failed, they hoped they might be able to wear down the enemy with guerrilla warfare.

All of these strategies, however, presumed the existence of a motivated fighting force. Commodore Matthew Perry, who commanded U.S. naval forces during the war, commented insightfully on the problem. "The Mexicans are not deficient in personal courage," he wrote; "nothing is wanting to make them good soldiers, other than military discipline and national ardor which cannot be expected of men impressed as they are into service, in the most cruel and ruthless manner."[1] The elites who managed the war tried mightily to convince themselves that the Mexican people clamored for a vindicating war, but in fact very few of those people were passionate about the fight. Nonelite Mexicans—the ones who were expected to do most of the fighting—realized that, in the eyes of their leaders, they were useful only as drudges or cannon fodder. During the war and its aftermath, when impoverished Mexicans fought enthusiastically, it was not against the foreign invaders but against their own overlords.

"National ardor" was also lacking among the elites themselves, making a unified response to the invasion practically impossible. Civil strife had become such an ingrained habit among Mexican politicos that not even a foreign invasion could keep them from fighting one another. "A sensible, patriotic people unites and offers a solid front at the first hint of the common peril," moaned one Mexican politician, even as U.S. forces closed in on Mexico City. "A people that is neither sensible nor patriotic grows weak, thus smoothing out difficulties for the invader, who wins without opposition."[2]

POLITICS AND WAR

During 1846, even as war with the United States loomed, Mexican politics remained tumultuous. Mariano Paredes had come to power in late 1845 as part of a conspiracy to convert Mexico to monarchy. He backed off of his monarchist pretensions upon becoming aware of how genuinely unpopular the notion of kingship was in Mexico. Still, the very threat of a return to such a despised system was enough to fire up the puros, who believed that a return to the federalist Constitution of 1824 was the ticket to victory in the war with the United States. Confident of this prescription, the puros became by far the most strident advocates of war. Indeed, they have the distinction of being virtually the only group that seemed actually to believe Mexico could win—but victory, in their view, would be possible only under the proper political system. Puro leader Valentín Gómez Farías was the most ardent champion of war and federalism. So intent was he on dumping Paredes that he was willing to deal with the devil. In 1846 he began a regular correspondence with his old nemesis, Antonio López de Santa Anna, who had been exiled from Mexico "for life" in 1845. Santa Anna was presently devoting himself to banquets and cockfights in Cuba. Gómez Farías believed that he and Santa Anna would make an unbeatable governing team: Gómez Farías claimed to have influence over the masses, while Santa Anna held sway with the army.

Gómez Farías was not Santa Anna's only potential route back to power. At the same time he was parleying with the Mexican puros, Santa Anna was also putting out feelers to their archenemies, the Americans. In February 1846 a U.S. citizen named Alejandro José Atocha visited President Polk claiming that Santa Anna had expressed a willingness, upon being restored to power, to make remarkable concessions: the Rio Grande boundary and all of modern-day New Mexico and northern California, in exchange for a $30 million indemnity. It was an attractive offer, but Atocha was a shady character. Polk was skeptical but was nevertheless persuaded that Santa Anna would be more conciliatory than Paredes. If some subtle way could be found to help Santa Anna make his political comeback, Polk was on board.

Meanwhile, Santa Anna assured Gómez Farías that during his Cuban sojourn he had become a liberal of conviction. Curiously, Gómez Farías seems to have found this plausible. A key feature of Santa Anna's genius was his impressive ability to persuade people that he was honest and sincere despite mountains of evidence to the contrary. Some Mexicans were themselves fairly mystified at their own continued willingness to trust the wily general. Moderate politician José Fernando Ramírez, who was normally of a very skeptical turn of mind, wrote to a friend, "There is no doubt whatsoever that [Santa Anna] is returning as a real democrat, and I can conceive of his being one." Ramírez, perhaps realizing how absurd that sounded, added laconically, "I cannot tell you on what I base my conviction."[3]

The liberals launched their rebellion in late July, even as U.S. forces were occupying California, preparing to occupy New Mexico, and plotting strategy in northern Mexico. When General José Mariano Salas joined the revolt in Mexico City, Paredes was finished. Paredes had been heading north to take charge of the army but was arrested en route. Salas became provisional president, but pending Santa Anna's return, Gómez Farías exercised the real power. In August 1846 the federalist Constitution of 1824 once again was declared to be the law of the land.

Santa Anna landed at Veracruz in August, apparently with the acquiescence of the American fleet that was blockading the Mexican coast. On Mexico's independence day, September 16, Gómez Farías and Santa Anna entered the capital together in an open carriage. The entry was deliberately low key, for the nation was in grave peril and the two leaders were resolved to appear as sober and sincere democrats. An enormous banner of the recently resurrected federalist constitution fluttered to the side of the carriage, but apart from that there were few decorations, and the two men were dressed in subtle civilian attire—no medals, no frock coats, nothing that might smack of aristocracy. According to Ramírez, they "seemed more like victims than conquerors."[4]

Ever the man of action, Santa Anna spent only two weeks in the capital before sallying northward at the head of three thousand ragged troops. In his absence he was elected president, and after some ugly politicking Gómez Farías became vice president, with power to govern while Santa Anna fought.

General Juan Alvarez, a caudillo of southern Mexico who was among the few bold enough to openly oppose the war with the United States, sized up the new regime's chief problem nicely. "Money, money, and more money," he wrote, "are the three things which are needed in order to recover [Texas], save California . . . and preserve our nationality."[5] Mexico's treasury, as usual, was bare, its normally meager revenues made more meager still by the U.S. blockade. The government decreed a barrage of emergency taxes and demanded contributions from the states and from urban property owners, but it lacked the means to collect such exactions or to deal with the fierce resistance they engendered.

The Catholic Church, with its apparent opulence, was as always a tempting place to look for funds. As a liberal of conviction, Gómez Farías was famously hostile toward the church, not merely for its wealth but because of the formidable obstacle it presented to the creation of a modern, liberal, secular nation-state. As he had done during his 1832–33 government, Gómez Farías attacked the church frontally. On January 11, 1847, he persuaded congress to authorize the government to raise 15 million pesos for the war effort by mortgaging or selling church property; he made exceptions for church schools, hospitals, and charities. The clergy loudly protested the measure, and they had plenty of support. Demonstrators threw stones at the National Palace, leaflets advocated death to congress and Gómez Farías, the churches of Mexico City suspended services in protest, and pulpits thundered with antigovernment jeremiads. Several states in the center of the country denounced the measure as ruinous not only to the church but to all those businesses, ranches, and farms that had borrowed money from church coffers. Zacatecas went so far as to advocate overthrowing the federal authorities and negotiating a quick end to the war with the United States, while the governor of San Luis Potosí asked the legislature to declare his state's independence from Mexico. There were even rumors that Zacatecas, Durango, Sinaloa, and Tabasco discussed declaring their independence from Mexico and asking for U.S. protection.

The crisis worsened when the puro governor of Mexico City, boldly declaring himself an atheist, sought to ignore some of the tax exemptions for charities and hospitals that had been mentioned in the January 11 law. In late February, when Gómez Farías ordered a conservative militia battalion—known as *los polkos* because of their fondness for dancing the polka—to prepare for the defense of Veracruz against an anticipated American invasion, the polkos refused to go. Instead, with moral and financial support from the church, they began a rebellion that plunged Mexico City into a condition just short of civil war. They denounced Gómez Farías for surrounding himself with the "most wretched and despicable [men] from among the dregs of all factions." They first demanded the repeal of the offensive tax laws and the dissolution of the executive and legislative branches of government but eventually said they would settle for the dismissal of Gómez Farías.

The polkos had little popular support. Many residents of the city did not fail to notice the appalling cynicism involved in sparking such an upheaval at the very moment when Mexican troops were battling the Americans in the north and when American forces were preparing to land at Veracruz for a march on the capital. The church seems to have lost some prestige because of its role in the polkos affair: few people turned out for the Holy Week celebrations later that year, and most did not even doff their hats out of respect as the religious processions passed by.

As had often happened previously in such situations, many looked to Santa Anna for salvation. At a critical moment Santa Anna abandoned the fight in the north and returned to Mexico City. People cheered and threw garlands of flowers in his path as he approached the city in late March. Just as he had done in 1833, Santa Anna now took the side of Gómez Farías's enemies: he persuaded the church to lend the government one and a half million pesos in exchange for the nullifi-

cation of the offending tax law, while at the same time he
withdrew his support from Gómez Farías. He pressured congress to simply abolish the office of vice president, and the
stubborn Gómez Farías had no recourse but to step down. A
Santa Anna crony, General Pedro María Anaya, became substitute president while Santa Anna prepared to continue
fighting the war.

THE NORTH AMERICAN INVASION

While the politicians wrangled, the war continued along its
disastrous course. In June 1846, only a month after the U.S.
declaration of war against Mexico, the Mexicans received the
unwelcome news that the United States and Great Britain,
after some moments of high tension, had patched up their
differences over the Oregon Territory. Many Mexicans had
hoped that that dispute might lead to war between Great
Britain and the United States, which could conceivably have
resulted in an Anglo-Mexican alliance. Instead, Britain rapidly lost interest in Mexico's plight, and the United States was
free to pursue its war with Mexico with one less distraction.

Zachary Taylor's army won victories at two battles just
north of the Rio Grande—Palo Alto and Resaca de la Palma—
in early May 1846, and his troops took Matamoros without
resistance. The Mexican forces withdrew to the city of Monterrey, about two hundred miles west of Matamoros. At that
point, hampered by the departure of volunteers serving short-
term enlistments and by lack of supplies, Taylor bided his
time until fresh troops and supplies arrived. On September 20
Taylor's forces laid siege to Monterrey, forcing the Mexicans
to capitulate after four days of fierce street fighting. A new
force under General John E. Wool linked up with those of
Taylor in February 1847, even as General Santa Anna was
taking over the Mexican war effort.

Santa Anna, upon returning to Mexico, had hastily as-

sembled an army practically without funding. He mortgaged
his own property, cobbled together his own resources, and
pressed the peons from his own haciendas into service. In San
Luis Potosí he seized bars of silver from the local mint, most
of which belonged to Spaniards. None of this was sufficient
to form a credible fighting force. Santa Anna's army had no
uniforms, little food, inferior weapons, and little training.
The lack of artillery and long-range rifles meant they could
fight only at close range, but the formidable U.S. artillery was
capable of slaughtering them ruthlessly at a comfortable distance, making it nearly impossible for the Mexicans to mount
an effective charge—a disadvantage that would cripple Mexican military efforts throughout the war. Statesmen in Mexico
City might make much of Mexican "honor," but for the rank-
and-file soldier national honor was a hopeless abstraction that
provided scant incentive for wanton self-sacrifice. And if
death on the field of battle seemed less than glorious, for
many such a death would have been a luxury: of the 20,000 or
so troops Santa Anna assembled at San Luis Potosí, nearly
five thousand perished of hunger, thirst, exhaustion, and ex-
posure during the grueling 240-mile march north to Saltillo.
Thousands more would die on the march back.

Even despite the appalling losses, Santa Anna's forces still
numbered some 15,000 upon reaching the environs of
Saltillo, where Taylor's men were encamped at a good defen-
sible position near a hacienda called Buena Vista. The Mexicans—hungry, exhausted, and demoralized as they were—still
had a decided numerical advantage, for Taylor had only
around 5,000 mostly green troops. Santa Anna was by this
time aware that the Americans were preparing an amphibious
invasion at Veracruz, and strategically it would have made
sense for him to refocus his efforts toward repelling that assault. But Santa Anna could not resist the temptation of enhancing his heroic stature by handing his enemy a glorious
trouncing. His army attacked on February 22 and again on

February 23, 1847. The fighting was intense and bloody. The Mexicans lost around 2,100 men, the Americans 673 plus some 1,500 desertions. Even with their terrible losses, the Mexicans retained a comfortable numerical advantage. Had Santa Anna chosen to renew the attack on February 24, the Mexicans might well have prevailed. But Santa Anna, persuaded that his army did not have enough food to hold out for another day, decided to withdraw his forces back to San Luis Potosí. The march back was probably as costly as a continuation of the battle would have been. By the time Santa Anna's army reached San Luis Potosí on March 12, he had lost more than half his original army of twenty thousand. The battle was reckoned an American victory, since it was the Mexicans who withdrew. Santa Anna suffered vicious criticism, including numerous charges of incompetence and treason, for his conduct of the campaign.

While the fighting raged in northern Mexico and political factions clashed in Mexico City, President Polk put into operation the next part of his plan—a move that had been under discussion for some time. Polk was persuaded that diplomacy and reason would not work with the Mexicans and that only a solid and indisputable rout would compel them to negotiate. He therefore appointed General Winfield Scott—a man he held in low esteem but whose military talents he appreciated—to head up an invasion of Mexico from the east. Scott's force of 12,000 landed south of Veracruz city on March 5, 1847, and invited the lightly defended city to surrender. Upon receiving a defiant reply, Scott ordered a bombardment that visited hellish destruction until the city surrendered on March 29. Anxious to move his forces inland before the heat of summer brought the scourge of yellow fever, Scott and his army set out almost immediately for the highlands.

The Americans, in their march from the coast, followed essentially the same route that the Spanish conquistador Hernán Cortés had followed more than three hundred years earlier. Both Cortés and Scott landed at Veracruz during Holy Week, making the historical parallel a bit eerie. The symbolism was not lost on either side in the conflict. The American soldiers were voracious readers of William H. Prescott's volume *History of the Conquest of Mexico*, published in 1843. They seem to have gained from that work a sense of historical and, perhaps, racial destiny, even while learning a bit about the Mexican landscape and archaeological remains. The Spanish conquest was again invoked when, after the war, General William J. Worth presented President Polk with a fine copy of a famous painting of Cortés. Although Polk frequently and vehemently denied that his war with Mexico was a war of conquest, he does not seem to have objected to the obvious symbolism of the gift: it first hung in the White House and currently hangs in Polk's ancestral home in Columbia, Tennessee.

On the Mexican side, some drew a dispiriting lesson from the conquest analogy. Five hundred years earlier a small crew of Spanish adventurers had been able to lay waste to an enormous empire because the people of Mexico failed to pull together against their common enemy. History seemed to be repeating itself. Other Mexicans sought to use the parallel more constructively: puros did their best to invoke Aztec imagery in hopes of instilling in the Mexican people some sense of racial pride and solidarity and to identify the hated Spaniards with the new conquerors.

Efforts to instill pride and patriotism in exhausted Mexican soldiers were fairly futile given the wretched and onerous conditions under which they were made to operate. Many of the troops who had fought at Buena Vista were now forcibly marched hundreds of miles southward, where, under the command of the indefatigable Santa Anna, they dug in to receive Scott's forces at a jagged mountain pass near the small town of Cerro Gordo. The position seemed well-nigh impregnable, surrounded as it was by a river, hills, and steep cliffs. The Mexican army had a small numerical advantage, with some twelve thousand troops to Scott's eighty-five hundred, but many of the Mexican soldiers were sick and exhausted. Others had been recently sprung from prison at Veracruz and pressed into service.

The Mexicans' numerical advantage counted for little against the Americans' superior ordnance, morale, and tactics. The Mexicans suffered a quick and decisive rout, as the U.S. forces seized huge quantities of Mexican munitions and took more than three thousand prisoners. Santa Anna's army collapsed; he himself was forced to flee on foot, losing the six-thousand-peso payroll for the troops in the process. The defeat at Cerro Gordo was especially demoralizing to Santa Anna, for it took place on his home turf, not far from his beloved haciendas.

After the Battle of Cerro Gordo, comparisons to the conquest grew starker and more disheartening. "The troops have come back very much depressed," wrote moderate politician José Fernando Ramírez. "The leaders and officers declare that the Yankees are invincible, and the soldiers are telling terrible tales that bring to mind the Conquest. Some say that the enemy soldiers are such huge, strong men that they can cut an opponent in two with a single sweep of their swords. It is also said that their horses are gigantic and very fast and that their muskets discharge shots which, once they leave the gun, divide into fifty pieces, each one fatal and well-aimed. Let us say nothing about their artillery, which has inspired fear and terror in all our troops and is undeniable proof of our backwardness in military art."[6]

In fact, however, Scott's army had its own problems. Some three thousand of his volunteers had enlisted for a year and were now free to go. On May 6, seven U.S. regiments marched off toward the coast to board ship for home. Another two thousand or so U.S. troops were wounded or gravely ill. Making matters still worse, on April 28, ten days after the Battle of Cerro Gordo, substitute president Pedro María Anaya issued a call for well-heeled patriots to form guerrilla units to disrupt the American supply lines along the Mexico City–Veracruz corridor. Other guerrilla units formed spontaneously and without government sanction. The guerrillas were quite successful in making life perilous for the Americans. Scott's army now consisted of fewer than five thousand healthy men, with no reinforcements expected and no reliable source of supplies.

General Scott—who, like Cortés, was gifted in both the military arts and those of diplomacy—was well aware of the dangers of widespread guerrilla warfare. He was also aware that the surest way to spawn guerrilla warfare was to mistreat ordinary Mexicans. He therefore carefully cultivated the goodwill of the common people by sternly disciplining any misbehavior on the part of his troops. He also wisely sought to appease the Roman Catholic clergy, ordering his soldiers to salute priests on the streets, requesting that priests celebrate mass with his troops, and personally attending mass in the opulent cathedrals of the cities. This strategy paid dividends: many top clergymen eagerly betrayed Santa Anna and made common cause with the invaders. Scott's forces were welcomed into the city of Puebla—a city some sixty miles southeast of Mexico City, known for its conservatism and piety—almost cordially, "more like travelers than enemies," in the words of the Spanish minister.

Scott spent a full three months at Puebla, plotting his assault on Mexico City. While he was there, a new character entered into the drama: upon learning of the seizure of Veracruz, Polk had dispatched a Spanish-speaking diplomat, Nicholas P. Trist, with authority to negotiate peace—presuming, of course, large territorial concessions—with the Mexicans. Trist had impeccable credentials, having studied law under Thomas Jefferson, married Jefferson's granddaughter, served as Andrew Jackson's private secretary, and been U.S.

consul to Cuba. Even so, Scott resented what he saw as Polk's effort to undercut his authority. He treated Trist coldly at first, though soon enough the two men became friendly. Trist was intrigued when the British minister informed him that Santa Anna had hinted that he would be susceptible to bribery—his price was ten thousand dollars down and another million once a treaty was ratified. Bribery was not only ethically dubious and sure to anger the administration in Washington; it was also an unreliable method of doing business, especially given Santa Anna's penchant for duplicity. With many reservations, General Scott approved the plan and provided the ten thousand dollars from his own funds for "secret expenses."

Nothing came of the bribery scheme. The Mexican congress had greeted news of the Mexican loss at the Battle of Cerro Gordo with a fresh round of defiance: two days after the battle they passed a law declaring it treasonous to so much as discuss treating with the enemy. Santa Anna claimed that this law obliged him to abandon negotiations with the U.S. agents—but not before he pocketed the ten thousand dollars. Santa Anna then told Trist that a U.S. attack on Mexico City would have the beneficial effect of frightening the opponents of peace into submission, enabling him to seize power and make peace. This interesting proposition clearly opened the way for a U.S. assault on the capital; the problem was, neither side was quite sure if the attack would be in earnest or for show.

The siege began August 20, 1847, with a pair of battles on the black craggy lava beds to the city's south. Once again the Mexican forces, though swelled by militiamen and even some Irish deserters from Scott's army, gave way before the superior U.S. firepower. The battles were costly to both sides, the Mexicans losing some four thousand men and the Americans more than a thousand. Sentiment among Mexican leaders in favor of surrender was by now considerable, but Santa Anna instead proposed a truce. Scott and Trist agreed and waited to see what sorts of concessions Santa Anna might make. The terms Santa Anna spelled out in a memo of August 26 were surprising: Mexico would recognize the independence of Texas, but with the Nueces as its southern border; the Americans must evacuate all occupied territory and raise the blockade of Mexico's ports; Mexico would consider granting the Americans some trading privileges in California; and the United States must pay all the costs of war, cancel all Mexican debts, and recognize all Mexican land grants in Texas made prior to 1836. With Mexican military fortunes at their lowest ebb, Santa Anna now proposed to end the war as though the Mexicans had won it.

Santa Anna's offer was rejected, of course, but negotiations still proceeded desultorily. All the while Santa Anna was allowing himself to be persuaded by those who advocated continued stubborn resistance. Perhaps the crowning absurdity of the matter was the ultimate sticking point: neither side was willing to barter away its preferred boundary for Texas. The virtually worthless territory between the Nueces and Rio Grande Rivers—a swath of land so arid it could not even support a cotton crop until the 1920s—was nonnegotiable for both sides. The Americans were determined to own the territory so as to maintain the fiction that the Mexicans had sparked the war by invading U.S. territory. Santa Anna believed the territory was essential as a buffer against future U.S. aggression. When the Mexican negotiators made it clear that they would not relinquish their demand for the Nueces boundary, and also that they had no intention of parting with New Mexico or southern California, the truce collapsed. Santa Anna had used the time to improve the city's defenses, in violation of the terms of the truce.

The fighting resumed on September 8 when the U.S. forces attacked an old flour mill known as the Molino del Rey, which they erroneously suspected of housing a cannon foundary. The Mexicans put up fierce resistance, engulfing the U.S. troops in a sustained hail of artillery fire, but after a two-hour fight the Mexican resistance collapsed. Before dawn on September 12 the Americans began shelling Chapultepec Castle, an imposing edifice that had once served as a residence for viceroys but that now served as Mexico's military academy. The castle, which rested on a hilltop some two hundred feet above the plain, guarded the western entrance to Mexico City. After a full day's bombardment the castle was badly damaged. On the morning of September 13 the bombardment resumed, followed by an assault. Specially selected U.S. troops used scaling ladders to climb the slopes, breach the castle walls, and engage the castle's defenders in brutal hand-to-hand combat. By nine-thirty in the morning, the castle had fallen to the Americans. The Battle of Chapultepec provided the ultimate symbol of Mexico's doomed resistance: six teenaged cadets, ordered to fall back, instead chose to fight to the death. One of the boys, according to patriotic legend, wrapped himself in the Mexican flag and leaped from the castle to his death rather than allow the flag to fall into American hands.

Late on the night after the Battle of Chapultepec, Santa Anna resigned the presidency of Mexico, gathered what was left of his army, and withdrew from the city. Shortly thereafter he besieged the tiny and ailing contingent that Scott had left at Puebla, but his army disintegrated as soon as U.S. reinforcements arrived. Santa Anna's midnight evacuation of Mexico City made him the object of much scorn and scapegoating. When he was summoned to a military court of inquiry, he resigned his military command and made his way into yet another exile.

On the morning of September 14 the American forces mustered in Mexico City's main square while a band played martial music and the Stars and Stripes were raised over the National Palace. Around midday General Scott rode into the square, resplendent in full-dress uniform, to accept the formal surrender of the city.

THE TREATY OF GUADALUPE HIDALGO

The surrender of Mexico City did not stop the fighting. The conflict simply devolved into something resembling class warfare, as the city's *léperos*—the urban poor so feared by the comfortable classes—joined by prisoners Santa Anna had ordered released from the city's jails, ransacked the National Palace and other public buildings. Even after the city seemed pacified, both the U.S. soldiers and city residents committed excesses and atrocities. Soldiers who ventured out into the streets, especially if they wandered from the city's center, were often shot from rooftops. On one occasion the corpses of several U.S. soldiers were found in a tavern where they had apparently been served poisoned pulque, the fermented maguey juice that was the favorite intoxicant of the Mexican poor. Many also fell victim to dysentery.

With the surrender of the city and the resignation of Santa Anna from the presidency, *ad interim* executive power fell to the chief justice of the Supreme Court, Manuel de la Peña y Peña. Peña y Peña relocated his government to the city of Querétaro, about one hundred miles to the north of Mexico City. There the politicians deliberated over whether to treat with the Americans or continue the war. They were as riven by faction as ever. Some felt the country's only hope of salvation lay in locating a European prince to assume the Mexican throne. Others maintained their loathing of monarchical government but had nevertheless come to the conclusion that Mexicans were incapable of governing themselves and would require outside assistance lest they succumb to the lawless passions of the "rabble." Some liberals favored making Mexico a protectorate of the United States, which would presumably restrain the power of the clergy, the monarchists, and the army while enhancing trade and bringing stability and progress to the country. Some puros went still further, favoring continuing the war until the United States agreed to outright annexation of the entire country.

A minority believed that Mexico might eventually prevail against the United States through guerrilla warfare. Most, however, were terrified by that prospect, for it would mean placing weapons and power in the hands of the unwashed masses and could morph into racial or class warfare. That, in turn, could end up consuming Mexico's privileged groups in the sort of hideous conflagration they had so long dreaded.

In the end, the Mexican elite's fear of the people proved decisive to the outcome of the war with the United States. The occupation of their country by a foreign power was, in the end, less unsettling than the specter of race war, which, they noted with great alarm, appeared already to be taking shape. The profound injustices of rural Mexico—a place where enormous haciendas monopolized the land, depriving or mercilessly exploiting Indian and mestizo peasants—meant that anger simmered and the threat of violent rebellion continually smoldered. In "normal" times suppressing rural discontent was a large part of the Mexican army's job. With the war the Mexican army was momentarily destroyed and the political elite in disarray. That created an opening that peasants in several regions of Mexico seized fervently.

In the far-off, perennially separatist state of Yucatán, Mayan Indians who had been mobilized by the white elite to fight on behalf of state autonomy charged that promises made to them in exchange for their military services were unfulfilled. They rose up against the peninsula's whites in what Yucatán's governor described as a "savage and exterminating war." "Everything is ravaged and destroyed," Governor Santiago Méndez wrote to U.S. secretary of state James Buchanan. "[T]he towns are delivered to flames, and all, without consideration of sex or age, who fall into the bloody hands of these barbarians, are murdered without pity, and with the most cruel tortures." The terrified whites knew they could expect no succor from Mexico: there was too much bad blood between Yucatán and central Mexico, and Mexico was in no condition to help in any case. In their desperation the Yucatecans implored the United States to intervene, offering in return nothing less than "dominion and sovereignty of the Country."[7] The United States declined the offer. This "Caste War of Yucatán" would come to rank among the most violent episodes in the history of the western hemisphere, costing the lives of some two-hundred thousand people in 1848 alone. By the time it wound down, the population of the Yucatán Peninsula had been reduced by half. Finally, in December 1848 Mexico was able to send some sixteen thousand troops to pacify the peninsula, a larger force than had ever been deployed during the war with the United States.

Meanwhile in the Sierra Gorda, a mountainous region comprised of parts of the states of Querétaro, Guanajuato, and San Luis Potosí, peasants using arms they had bought cheaply from U.S. troops at Tampico had been rebelling violently against war taxes since 1846. In 1847 they joined their tax and agrarian demands to a demand for war without quarter against the Americans. By the end of 1847 the movement was growing more violent still under the leadership of a Mexican army deserter named Eleuterio Quiroz. Peasant revolts were also ongoing in Puebla, San Luis Potosí, the Huasteca region of Veracruz, and Tamaulipas, where local archives and haciendas were torched, judges and landowners killed. Even more than usual Mexico appeared to be spinning wildly out of control. Ending the war with the United States was essential to containing race and class violence—that, at least, was something most Mexican politicians could agree on. Toward the end of 1847 the Mexican congress managed to elect General Pedro María Anaya, a former henchman of Santa Anna's but a man of moderate tendencies, to the presidency. Anaya, in turn, commissioned a trio of commissioners to negotiate a peace with the United States. The negotiations began in earnest in January 1848. The Mexicans thus acknowledged their loss of the war. It only remained to be seen how much territory they would lose in the bargain.

On the U.S. side, some were encouraged by Mexico's ongoing misfortunes. U.S. negotiator Nicholas Trist, seeing the desperation of the elite Mexicans at the continuing violence and social disintegration of their country, fell prey to the same sort of myopic American exceptionalism that had made Joel Poinsett such anathema to Mexican nationalists: he became convinced that the notion of annexing all of Mexico to the United States had widespread and enthusiastic support among Mexicans, at least among the "best part" of the population. What the United States encountered in the wake of the war was, Trist enthused, a "phenomenon altogether unexampled in the history of the world: a nation [the United States], to whose principles & habits & institutions the spirit of conquest is altogether foreign, actually has thrust upon her, by its own inhabitants, the acquisition of a country, rich beyond calculation in numberless sources of commercial prosperity, & abounding in every thing that can make a country desirable." For Trist, even the most passionate statements of defiance seemed to confirm the Mexicans' secret desire to relinquish their nation.[8]

Those Mexicans who favored joining the United States would likely have had second thoughts had they been aware of the kind of rhetoric that swirled around this option in the United States. There was indeed a movement pushing for U.S. acquisition of all of Mexico. For some, news of U.S. military successes was an occasion to indulge in a giddy spree of racial self-congratulation. In early 1847 a writer for the *Democratic Review* predicted optimistically, "The Mexican race now see, in the fate of the aborigines of the north, their own inevitable destiny. They must amalgamate and be lost, in the superior vigor of the Anglo-Saxon race, or they must utterly perish."[9] The New York *Globe* was still more to the point: "There is a spirit abroad which will not long be stayed—a spirit of progress, which will compel us, for the good of both nations and the world at large, TO DESTROY THE NATIONALITY *of that besotted people*. It would almost seem that they, like the Israelites of old, had brought upon themselves the vengeance of the Almighty and we ourselves had been raised up to overthrow AND UTTERLY DESTROY THEM *as a separate and distinct nation*."[10]

Some in the United States, of course, decried such sentiments as immoral and arrogant imperialist fantasies. But the arguments that eventually carried the day against the "All Mexico" movement were essentially racist ones. Ironically, southern slave owners, who before the war had been among the most aggressive expansionists, were at the forefront of the opposition to the movement. Mexico had a long history of hostility to slavery, so its incorporation as a free state would have immensely strengthened the antislavery forces. Opponents of the All Mexico movement also argued that Mexico contained entirely too many Mexicans—a people they had long denounced as a vicious, ignorant, slothful, uncivilized, "mongrel" race. Making such people citizens of the Union would be offering them a distinction they did not merit; such people, rather than allowing themselves to be uplifted by the Anglo-Saxons, just might end up dragging the Anglos down to their level. John C. Calhoun, ardent expansionist and defender of slavery, emerged as perhaps the most vocal opponent of acquiring all of Mexico. The United States, he said, had never incorporated nonwhite people as citizens. "Ours is a government of the white man," he told Congress, and to place nonwhites on an equal plane with whites would be a "fatal error."[11] It would be better, Calhoun and others of his ilk concluded, to take over only the sparsely inhabited regions of Mexico's far north.

The All Mexico movement was of little consequence in the end. Nicholas Trist, despite his enthusiasm for taking over the entire country, based his peace negotiations on what President Polk had said he wanted. The negotiations were not without friction. Back in October President Polk, upon learning of the failure of negotiations during the truce preceding the assault on Mexico City, had ordered Trist to abandon his mission and return to the United States. Since communication between Washington and Mexico took from three weeks to a month in transit, Trist did not learn of his recall until November 16. By that time the Mexican government, controlled by moderates, was clearly disposed to negotiate. Trist therefore resolved to disregard the order for his recall and press ahead with negotiations.

From there the negotiations went relatively smoothly and quickly. By the end of January the Mexicans had agreed to nearly all of the demands that Polk had insisted upon in his original instructions to Trist. They were willing to accept the Rio Grande as the boundary of Texas, and a border for New Mexico and California running from El Paso to the Pacific at the thirty-second parallel. The United States would assume all of the debts it claimed Mexico owed to U.S. citizens and pay an indemnity of $15 million for New Mexico and California—some $10 million less than the United States had been willing to spend before the war. The territory in question comprised over 525,000 square miles, about 55 percent of Mexico's land. It would eventually be divided into the states of Texas, California, and Utah, most of New Mexico and Arizona, and parts of Colorado and Wyoming. Trist and the Mexican commissioners signed the treaty on February 2 at the town of Guadalupe Hidalgo, very near the shrine of Mexico's patron saint, the Virgin of Guadalupe.

Polk, though enraged by Trist's act of insubordination and deeply ensconced in second thoughts about just how much territory the United States should acquire from Mexico, could not find a face-saving way of quashing the treaty, inasmuch as it granted everything he had claimed to be seeking at the outset of the war. To oppose the treaty now that it was a fait accompli would be rank hypocrisy, especially given his repeated insistence that the war with Mexico had not been a war of conquest. Polk considered Trist to be "destitute of honour or principle . . . a very base man," but he nevertheless forwarded the treaty to Congress. After some contentious debate it was approved on March 10. Mexico's congress ratified the treaty on March 30. In mid-June U.S. troops began their evacuation of Mexico City, and by the end of July Mexico was entirely free of foreign occupation.

EPILOGUE AND CONCLUSION

The war between the United States and Mexico had far-reaching consequences for both of the countries involved, and it profoundly affected relations among the nations of the western hemisphere. The most obvious consequences of the war, of course, were that many people died and an enormous amount of territory changed hands. Casualty figures for the United States are reasonably reliable: some 13,780 died, although fewer than 1,800 were killed in combat, the rest succumbing to disease. Many more were gravely wounded, and more still perished in the years following the war from diseases contracted in Mexico. The figures on the Mexican side are harder to come by. One common estimate says that some 25,000 died, though other estimates place the toll at twice that number.

The territorial transfer unleashed toxic political passions that a little over a decade later would plunge both the United States and Mexico into bloody civil wars. The U.S.-Mexican War exacerbated the imbalance in wealth and power that had,

in large measure, caused it in the first place, and that imbalance has yet to be corrected. The lingering resentments
caused by the war can be felt even in the present day.

THE CONSEQUENCES

President James K. Polk was convinced that slavery had no
relevance to territorial expansion. In fact, however, there was
a widespread conviction among both pro- and antislavery
forces that slavery would inevitably find its way into the
newly acquired territory, the two sides differing only in their
assessment of how desirable that was. From the beginning of
the annexation movement in 1844, Whigs had denounced
expansion as a conspiracy to extend slavery and hence to increase the power of slave owners.

In the hope of addressing the problem, a first-term congressman from Pennsylvania named David Wilmot had, in
1846, attempted to attach a proviso to the bill appropriating
funds for the war with Mexico. It said that "as an express and
fundamental condition of the acquisition of any territory
from the Republic of Mexico . . . neither slavery nor involun-
tary servitude shall ever exist in any part of said territory."
Debate over the proviso divided northern and southern wings
of the Democratic Party, in effect destroying the party
and converting party loyalties into sectional loyalties. The
Wilmot Proviso was defeated in the Senate, where southern
Democrats were strong, and its demise made plain the severe
damage that the issue of slavery was inflicting on U.S. culture
and institutions. Many southerners had long seen slavery as a
necessary evil. Now, finding themselves on the defensive, they
began to revise their views, tending increasingly to maintain
that slavery was a positive good for everyone involved and a
hard-won and absolute right for the slave owner. As a group
of Alabamians asked rhetorically in 1846, "When the war-
worn soldier returns to his home, is he to be told that he can-

not carry his property to the country won by his blood, or purchased by his money?"[1]

Efforts to smooth over the controversy proved ineffective. A "compromise" hammered out in 1850 admitted California as a free state while placing no restrictions on slavery in the newly organized territories of New Mexico, Nevada, Arizona, and Utah. At the same time the Fugitive Slave Act was passed to appease southerners, making it easier for slave owners to recapture escaped slaves. These mere stopgap measures satisfied no one but rather made both sides all the more resolved to defend their positions and extend their power.

The growing divisions were reflected in a major change in attitudes toward territorial aggrandizement. After 1850 Manifest Destiny became Sectional Destiny, as southerners mounted, encouraged, or financed filibustering expeditions— that is, armed expeditions by privateers, unsanctioned by the government—to seize territory in Mexico, the Caribbean, and Central America. One such expedition, led by Tennessee physician William Walker, managed to take over Nicaragua and govern it from 1855 to 1857, legalizing slavery in hopes of attracting southern immigrants. Northern foes of slavery, naturally, became resolute anti-imperialists.

The lands acquired from Mexico, then, sharpened the sectional divide and contributed greatly to the tensions that sparked the U.S. Civil War in 1861. Justo Sierra, a prominent statesman of the late nineteenth and early twentieth centuries, found a certain wry satisfaction in this: Mexico, he wrote, has had "a sort of malign influence on its invaders which would seem to have some mysterious relation to justice. French intervention in Mexico led to the Franco-Prussian war; American invasion led to the War Between the States."[2]

The U.S.-Mexican War, in addition to increasing sectional rivalries, led to another enduring tension in U.S. society. When the Treaty of Guadalupe Hidalgo was signed, there were very roughly one hundred thousand Spanish-speaking Mexican citizens in the territory that became the southwestern United States. Those people were given several options: they could move to Mexico and retain their Mexican citizenship; they could remain in the United States and retain their Mexican citizenship; or they could remain in the United States and gain full U.S. citizenship rights at some future time that was left unspecified. The majority chose the last option. Hispanics quickly became an ethnic minority in their native land, and as such they were lumped together with blacks and Indians, people whose civil rights were ambiguous and routinely abused. Predictably, the ink was hardly dry on the Treaty of Guadalupe Hidalgo before the first episodes of mob violence against Mexicans began to occur, especially in the volatile society of California during the Gold Rush. There were also abuses involving property rights. Some Hispanic families held imperfect title to their lands. The U.S. Senate had rejected a proposed clause to the Treaty of Guadalupe Hidalgo that would have automatically legitimized such titles, so titleholders were forced to fight for their lands in the U.S. courts. During the ensuing decades many found themselves despoiled. During the 1960s and 1970s organizations arose to demand that the civil rights of *chicanos*—as they began styling themselves at that time—be fully respected and that their lands be restored to them.

While much of this story is no doubt somewhat familiar to most Americans, the impact of the War of 1847 on Mexico is surely less well appreciated. The war brought Mexico to new depths of material and spiritual devastation. While peasant rebellions shook the provinces, the cities continued their morbid decline. In 1850 the country was ravaged by yet another plague of cholera, which was worsened by the chronic poverty in which much of the population lived. In Mexico City fetid marshlands became such fearsome breeding grounds for the bacteria that people shut themselves and their families up in their tiny homes, afraid even to eat or to open the doors to let the air in.

Highly partisan newspapers, broadsides, and pamphlets also continued to proliferate, and their tone became ever more strident, the positions more rigid, as both liberals and conservatives interpreted Mexico's defeat as the final confirmation of the positions they had long maintained and of the wrongness of their opponents' views. In making their cases, liberals and conservatives rounded up the usual suspects. For liberals, the fundamental problem remained the enormous gap between rich and poor and between the productive and the parasitic classes. Mexico's grievous problems, said the liberals, included parish priests who preyed upon the poor, exacting exorbitant fees for performing sacraments while assuring the poor of a heavenly reward; and upper clergy, who lived in luxury while refusing to defend the country, even cavorting shamelessly with the enemy. The church was an economic liability also, for it refused to pay its fair share toward the commonweal even while impeding progress in agriculture by monopolizing and perversely underutilizing three-quarters of the country's arable land. The army—another favorite bugbear of liberals—had displayed the full measure of its incompetence and corruption to the entire world. Wealthy Mexicans, for their part, refused to pay taxes while perpetuating the aristocratic notion that productive labor was degrading.

For liberals, the solution was thoroughgoing reform, which would bring the country fully into the modern world and jettison all that smacked of colonial times. This idea was not exactly new, of course, but a new generation was coming into its own, and they would soon raise the stakes of the struggle. Confident, self-assured, and uncompromising men like Benito Juárez, Melchor Ocampo, Guillermo Prieto, and

Ponciano Arriaga first made their mark around the time of the war, and they would soon come into control of the nation's destiny.

For their part, conservatives viewed the loss of the war as the final and most indisputable proof that republican institutions were ill suited to Mexican reality and that only a strong and unmolested church and a stable monarchy could restore order to the country. Back in 1840 José María Gutiérrez de Estrada had caused an enormous stir when he published a pamphlet advocating monarchy for Mexico. With the loss of the war, Gutiérrez's ideas were revived and aired unapologetically. Mexico had been peaceful, prosperous, and stable as a Spanish colony, the conservatives argued, and the reasons should be clear to all: it had had a strong church safeguarding the people's morals, and a king who was respected by people of every class, race, and region. Republicanism had put power into unworthy hands, conservatives insisted, and federalism exacerbated the problems inspired by Mexico's diversity and regionalism.

The ideological dispute built gradually to a crescendo in the years following the war. For five years after the Treaty of Guadalupe Hidalgo moderates governed Mexico under the federalist Constitution of 1824. The postwar economic depression and the continuing upheavals in the cities and countryside gave critics of the government plenty of ammunition. The country's economic problems were intractable enough to defeat fourteen finance ministers in the three years after 1848. By the spring of 1851 the American indemnity payment was entirely spent, and the treasury was bare once again.

The first postwar president, José Joaquín de Herrera (1848–51), had the distinction of being the first in Mexico's history to complete a full term in office and hand power to a legally elected successor. Even so, the constitutional order remained shaky. The crisis gathered momentum during 1852, as conservatives and moderates, convinced that only a king or dictator could control the country, plotted to overthrow the government. The leader of the rebellion, Colonel José María Blancarte, rose up in Guadalajara with a surprising demand: that General Antonio López de Santa Anna be raised once again to power.

At the end of war Santa Anna had fled Mexico in disgrace, dogged by charges of treason. He had been spending his exile in Cartagena, Colombia, where he had acquired substantial properties and was living quite comfortably with his young wife. The aging dean of conservatism, Lucas Alamán, tried to make clear in a letter to Santa Anna that, while he would be granted broad powers to restore order, he would be expected to govern on "conservative principles." That is, he must respect and protect the Catholic Church and its religion, maintain a strong army, and defer to the hombres de bien. Moderate liberal President Mariano Arista resigned on January 5, 1853, and Santa Anna was elected overwhelmingly. He formally took over the office of president for the eleventh and last time on April 20.

Unfortunately, Lucas Alamán died only a few weeks after Santa Anna's installation as president. With Alamán out of the way, Santa Anna was free to indulge all his most imperious and intemperate instincts. He officially suspended the 1824 Constitution on his second day in office and thereafter governed with no constitution at all and with no apparent intention of ever providing one. He surrounded himself with sycophants, lived luxuriously, insisted upon the title His Most Serene Highness, gave himself power to shut down any periodical he disliked, employed a secret police force to hunt down critics, lavished money on the army without significantly reforming it, and kowtowed to the clergy. To help pay for his extravagances, he sold the Mesilla Valley, more than forty-five thousand square miles of Mexican land below the New Mexico and Arizona borders, to the United States for a railroad right of way. Mexicans were outraged.

Santa Anna, in the words of historian John Lynch, "suffered from a permanent inability to see things as they were."[3] Imagining himself an immensely popular enlightened despot, he was surprised by the ferocity of the rebellion that erupted in 1854 and triumphed in 1855. The new generation of liberals that was ushered in by this rebellion began a program of reform that exceeded the wildest dreams of Valentín Gómez Farías, and it provoked a violent response from conservatives. The upshot was the bloodiest civil war Mexico had yet seen, the so-called War of the Reform, which raged from 1858 to 1861, after which Mexico had to face yet another foreign invasion, this time by the French. The country would not experience stability until the last quarter of the nineteenth century.

The war between the United States and Mexico, then, had crucial domestic consequences for both countries. It also had long-lasting effects on relations between the United States and Mexico, and by extension between the United States and all of Latin America. Latin Americans had been wary of the growing power of the United States from its inception, but the U.S.-Mexican War seemed to confirm their view that the United States was a devious, domineering, meddling, arrogant, and aggressive imperialist power, one that threatened the very existence of its hemispheric neighbors. This opinion has been frequently reinforced by the United States' numerous later interventions in the internal affairs of Latin American countries, many of them involving armed force. The United States and Mexico, moreover, explicitly agreed in Article 21 of the Treaty of Guadalupe Hidalgo to renounce war as a means of settling disputes. If disputes could not be resolved through normal diplomatic channels, then both countries agreed they would submit them to bilateral commissions for arbitration. Despite this clause, the United States has carried out two major armed incursions into Mexico (in 1914 and 1916) and a number of minor ones. Several disputes have been submitted to arbitration, and while Mexico has a good record of abiding by arbitrated decisions, the United States has tended to disregard them.

The experience of losing a war to the United States helped to forge what has traditionally been the keystone of Mexico's foreign policy—that is, a passionate adherence to the principles of nonintervention and respect for national sovereignty. Mexico has not only taken a hard line against U.S. intervention in Mexico itself; it has been at the forefront of denouncing U.S. meddling throughout the hemisphere and the world. In recent years Mexico has cited the nonintervention principle to denounce U.S. meddling in Central America and Cuba (with which Mexico has, to the annoyance of the United States, generally maintained cordial relations) and to oppose U.S. plans for the invasion of Iraq. Mexico, like other Latin American countries, has tended to alternate between open defiance of and cooperation with the United States, but an undercurrent of tension and mistrust has been a constant.

The U.S.-Mexican War also created a new border nearly two thousand miles in length. During the century and a half since the war, the U.S.-Mexican borderland has become a world unto itself, a source of many international problems and disputes, from Indian raids to drug smuggling to pollution to labor abuse to illegal immigration. Most of those difficulties are, of course, the result of the immensity of the border and the dramatic inequality in wealth between the two countries, a problem that the war did nothing to resolve.

WHY MEXICO WENT TO WAR

An enduring myth holds that the Mexicans went to war with the United States because they were drunk on a noxious cocktail of obstinacy, vanity, pride, shortsightedness, and naïveté. According to this version, the Mexicans more or less deliberately provoked the United States into declaring war—

a view no doubt influenced by the peculiar spin President Polk gave the matter—convinced they could either win or produce enough bluster to impel the United States to back down.

Certainly it is not hard to find examples of Mexican bluster and bellicosity, but the great irony and tragedy of the war lies in the fact that nearly all Mexicans in a position to make decisions realized full well that entering war with the United States was folly and that Mexico's loss was a foregone conclusion. Mariano Arista, commander of Mexican troops at the northern border, in his private correspondence, described his army's lack of resources as "absolute." The troops were badly clothed and armed and fed, horses were few, and there was no money to pay the troops or to hire scouts and spies. If Mexico went to war, Arista wrote in the fall of 1845, it would surely be "defeated and dominated by Americans."[4] For their part, both Herrera and Paredes refused to declare war, insisting that any fighting Mexico did would be purely defensive. Both searched vainly for an honorable exit from this predicament.

In the end, Mexico went to war with the United States not in spite of its weakness but *because* of its weakness. Had Mexico been a great deal stronger and more unified, it would not have encountered such difficulty in populating, controlling, and defending its northern territories, and it could therefore have presented a more formidable obstacle to U.S. territorial ambitions. Had Mexico been just a *bit* stronger and more unified, it might have been possible for politicians to make decisions on the basis of rational calculation rather than raw political passion. But in a country whose early history was a depressing litany of frustration; in a country where both liberals and conservatives had had the opportunity to test their policies and encountered only failure; in a country crippled by divisions of class, race, region, and ideology; in a country that could make a hero out of a vainglorious opportunist like Santa Anna; in such a country, "honor" became paramount.

While very few Mexicans in public life truly believed Mexico could win a war with the United States—and many doubted it could even *survive* such a war—anyone who voiced this opinion was invariably attacked as a traitor and a coward.

Texas was the crucible. From the time of the Texas separatist revolt, politicians of all stripes—the desperate, the demagogic, the demented, and the well-intentioned—had made Texas a symbol of what threatened Mexico's nationality. Unable to accept the failure of their policies, their tendency was to blame the loss of Texas on the perfidy of the United States and the foolishness of their political rivals. The loss of Texas proved to both ideological factions that their antagonists' prescriptions were ruinous. Conservatives charged that liberals, instead of abiding by proven tradition, had weakened Mexico by slavishly imitating the ideas and institutions of the United States, opening the way for ignorant and irresponsible people to assert their will. Liberals responded that if the conservative regimes in Mexico City had allowed greater freedom and representation at the local level, the Texans would have had no cause to rebel; and that if the institutions of conservatism—the church and the army—had not monopolized so many of the nation's resources, Mexico would have had the wherewithal to defend its territory. In the words of one prominent moderate politician, Texas became a "weapon that each of the quarreling factions wants to get hold of in order to wound its opponents to the death. The first one who talks about peace will lose that weapon, and, therefore, no one wants to utter the fateful word."[5]

As with most enduring feuds, pride and vanity were factors. To seek compromise with political enemies was a sign of weakness: enemies had to be bested and destroyed. Curiously, this attitude had both internecine and international dimensions. In its international manifestation, it was ironically a source of some rare unity. All factions agreed that Texas must be won back and that a failure to do so would be a permanent stain on Mexico's national honor. Compromise with the foreigners was a sign of weakness, and as such any apparent movement in that direction was cause for outrage. Thus many highly intelligent Mexicans privately offered bleak assessments of Mexico's chances in a war with the United States while at the same time making brazen statements for public consumption. General Mariano Arista, immediately after declaring Mexico's situation virtually hopeless, issued a stirring denunciation of the United States and all it represented, and he called on all Mexicans to "defend not only the honor and decorum of the nation but also the territory, the nationality and the existence of Mexico as an independent republic."[6] General Manuel de Mier y Terán, the man who tried so desperately to retain Texas for Mexico, lamented that Texas was irrevocably lost and Mexico's nationality gravely threatened, while at the same time he denounced anyone who would consent to the loss of Texas as "an execrable traitor who ought to be punished with every kind of death."[7]

War with the United States also permitted the politicians to indulge the illusion that the Mexican people were resolute and united against the foreign foe. But their illusions were belied by the overwhelming indifference with which most Mexicans responded to the call to arms. While in the United States a call for volunteer militiamen was answered so enthusiastically that many volunteers had to be turned away, Mexico had to fill its ranks by rounding up vagabonds. The war with the United States not only failed to inspire unity among Mexicans, it also illustrated the tragic depths of the nation's disunity: the war created an opening for the poor and oppressed to rise in rebellion. Mexican elites, soon after the war's end, purchased guns at bargain prices from the United States, which they used to put down those rebellions. The war, in the end, only caused a further unraveling of an already-broken nation.

Given Mexico's condition in 1846, it would have made

sense to negotiate for a handsome indemnity payment in exchange for ceding territories that Mexico clearly could not control. But the rational strategy was unacceptable for two reasons: it would have been tantamount to recognizing the right of the United States to expand its boundaries almost at will, imposing its racist vision everywhere; and it would have necessitated compromise with political opponents. Given those realities, the desperate glory of death on the battlefield seemed preferable to the ignominy of compromise and surrender. As one newspaper put it, "Defeat and death on the Sabine would be glorious and beautiful," much preferable to an "infamous and execrable" peace.[8] In a sense Mexico's statesmen resolved to face war in the same spirit as General Terán had done in 1832 when he dressed in his finery and fell on his sword. They chose to suffer a glorious defeat.

NOTES

PREFACE

1. Greensboro *News & Record*, May 11, 2003.
2. John Ross, "Proxy Soldiers in Bush's War: Mexico Fiercely Opposes the Iraq War, But Mexicans Are Dying There Every Week," *La Prensa–San Diego*, August 17, 2004.
3. *Personal Memoirs of U.S. Grant*, vol. 1 (New York: Charles L. Webster & Co., 1885), 53.
4. Quoted in *Texas Journal of Commerce*, July 10, 1880.

1. THE UNITED STATES AND MEXICO, CIRCA 1821

1. Alexis De Tocqueville: *Democracy in America*, ed. J. P. Mayer, tr. George Lawrence (New York: HarperPerennial, 1969), 165.
2. Ibid., 9.
3. Brantz Mayer, *Mexico as It Was and as It Is* (New York: J. Winchester, 1844), 41.
4. Alexander von Humboldt, *Political Essay on the Kingdom of New Spain*, ed. Mary Maples Dunn, tr. John Black (Norman: University of Oklahoma Press, 1972), 64.
5. Quoted in R. R. Palmer, *The Age of Democratic Revolution: A Political History of Europe and America, 1760–1800* (Princeton, 1959), 192.
6. Quoted in Charles Hale, "The War with the United States and the Crisis in Mexican Thought," *Americas* 14, no. 2 (October 1957), 168.
7. Rice Vaughan, *A Discourse of Coin and Coinage* (London, 1675), quoted in Joyce Appleby, "The Social Origins of American

Revolutionary Ideology," *Journal of American History* 64, no. 4 (March 1978), 945.

8. John H. Coatsworth, "Obstacles to Economic Growth in Nineteenth-Century Mexico," *American Historical Review* 83 (1978), 85.

2. THINGS FALL APART

1. Quoted in David Brading, *The First America: The Spanish Monarchy, Creole Patriots, and the Liberal State, 1492–1867* (Cambridge: Cambridge University Press, 1991), 599–600.
2. Quoted in Frederick Merk, *Manifest Destiny and Mission in American History* (New York: Vintage Books, 1963), 28.
3. Jefferson to Archibald Stuart, January 25, 1786, in *The Life and Selected Writings of Thomas Jefferson*, ed. Adrienne Koch and William Peden (New York: Modern Library, 1944), 391.
4. Quoted in Lars Schoultz, *Beneath the United States: A History of U.S. Policy Toward Latin America* (Cambridge, Mass.: Harvard University Press, 1998), 5.
5. Quoted in David J. Weber, *The Mexican Frontier, 1821–1846: The American Southwest Under Mexico* (Albuquerque: University of New Mexico Press, 1982), 160.
6. Quoted in Eugene C. Barker, *The Life of Stephen F. Austin, Founder of Texas, 1793–1836* (New York: AMS Press, 1970), 38.
7. Quoted in Gregg Cantrell, *Stephen F. Austin: Empresario of Texas* (New Haven, Conn.: Yale University Press, 1999), 130.
8. Quoted in J. Fred Rippy, *Joel R. Poinsett, Versatile American* (Durham, N.C.: Duke University Press, 1935), 18.
9. Ibid., 293.
10. Stanley C. Green, *The Mexican Republic: The First Decade, 1823–1832* (Pittsburgh: University of Pittsburgh Press, 1987), 161.

3. THE PROBLEM OF TEXAS

1. Quoted in Ohland Morton, *Terán and Texas: A Chapter in Texas-Mexican Relations* (Austin: Texas State Historical Association, 1948), 55.
2. José María Sánchez, "A Trip to Texas in 1828," *Southwestern Historical Quarterly* 29, no. 4 (April 1926), 283.
3. Terán to governor of Coahuila y Tejas, June 24, 1828, in Terán,

Texas by Terán: The Diary Kept by General Manuel de Mier y Terán on His 1828 Inspection of Texas, ed. Jack Johnson, tr. John Wheat (Austin: University of Texas Press, 2000), 94.

4. Sánchez, "Trip to Texas," 271.

5. Terán, *Texas by Terán*, 101.

6. Sánchez, "Trip to Texas," 279.

7. Terán, *Texas by Terán*, 33, 178.

8. This famous letter is quoted at great length in Alleine Howren, "Causes and Origin of the Decree of April 6, 1830," *Southwestern Historical Quarterly* 16, no. 4 (April 1913), 400–01.

9. Terán quoted in ibid., 400.

10. Sánchez, "Trip to Texas," 261.

11. Diario del Gobierno, August 5, 1837, quoted in Michael Costeloe, *The Central Republic in Mexico, 1835–1846: Hombres de Bien in the Age of Santa Anna* (Cambridge: Cambridge University Press, 1993), 24.

12. Quoted in Timothy Anna, *Forging Mexico, 1821–1835* (Lincoln: University of Nebraska Press, 1998), 231.

13. Quoted in Douglas T. Miller, *The Birth of Modern America, 1820–1850* (New York: Pegasus, 1970), 39.

14. Quoted in Terán, *Texas by Terán*, 186.

4. SANTA ANNA AND THE TEXAS REVOLUTION

1. Quoted in Gregg Cantrell, *Stephen F. Austin, Empresario of Texas* (New Haven, Conn.: Yale University Press, 1999), 259.

2. Quoted in Wilfrid Hardy Callcott, *Santa Anna: The Story of an Enigma Who Once Was Mexico* (Norman: University of Oklahoma Press, 1936), 108–9.

3. Brantz Mayer, *Mexico as it Was and as It Is* (New York: J. Winchester, 1844), 73.

4. Fanny Calderón de la Barca, *Life in Mexico* (Berkeley: University of California Press, 1982), 45.

5. Austin to Samuel M. Williams, March and April 1832, quoted in Eugene C. Barker, *The Life of Stephen F. Austin, Founder of Texas, 1793–1836: A Chapter in the Westward Movement of the Anglo-American People* (Austin: University of Texas Press, 1926), 386.

6. Austin to Williams, October 6, 1834, quoted in ibid., 445.

7. Santa Anna to secretary of war and marine, February 1, 1836,

quoted in James Presley, "Santa Anna in Texas: A Mexican Viewpoint," *Southwestern Historical Quarterly* 62:4 (April 1959), 494.

8. Austin to L.F. Linn, May 4, 1836, quoted in Cantrell, *Empresario*, 344.

9. Quoted in Terán, *Texas by Terán*, 186.

10. Quoted in David J. Weber, *The Mexican Frontier, 1821–1846: The American Southwest Under Mexico* (Albuquerque: University of New Mexico Press, 1982), 246.

5. THE ELUSIVE RECONQUEST

1. Fanny Calderón de la Barca, *Life in Mexico* (Berkeley: University of California Press, 1982), 452.

2. Quoted in George Rives, *The United States and Mexico, 1821–1848*, 2 vols. (New York: Charles Scribner's Sons, 1913), 1:469.

3. Quoted in Stanley Siegel, *A Political History of the Texas Republic, 1836–1845* (Austin: University of Texas Press, 1956), 73.

4. Quoted in ibid., 148.

5. José María de Bocanegra to Waddy Thompson, August 23, 1843, in *Diplomatic Correspondence of the United States: Inter-American Affairs, 1831–1860*, ed. William R. Manning, 12 vols. (Washington: Carnegie Endowment for International Peace, 1937), 8:557.

6. Quoted in Michael Costeloe, *The Central Republic in Mexico, 1835–1846: Hombres de Bien in the Age of Santa Anna* (Cambridge: Cambridge University Press, 1993), 245.

6. THE ANNEXATION CRISIS

1. Quoted in Justin Smith, *The Annexation of Texas* (New York: AMS Press, 1971; reprinted from 1911 edition), 145.

2. Quotations from O'Sullivan and *New York Morning News* from Frederick Merk, *Manifest Destiny and Mission in American History: A Reinterpretation* (New York: Vintage, 1963), 25 and 31–32.

3. Quoted in George Rives, "Mexican Diplomacy on the Eve of War with the United States," *American Historical Review* 28 (October–July 1913), 278.

4. Quoted in ibid., 282.

5. Quoted in Thomas Hietala, *Manifest Design: American Excep-*

tionalism and Empire, rev. ed. (Ithaca, N.Y.: Cornell University Press, 1985), xiii.

6. Quoted in Michael Costeloe, *The Central Republic in Mexico, 1835–1846: Hombres de Bien in the Age of Santa Anna* (Cambridge: Cambridge University Press, 1993), 269.

7. José Fernando Ramírez, *Mexico During the War with the United States*, ed. Walter V. Scholes, tr. Elliott B. Scherr (Columbia: University of Missouri Studies, 1950), 124.

8. Brantz Mayer, *Mexico as it Was and as It Is* (New York: J. Winchester, 1844), 4.

9. Ramírez, *Mexico During the War*, 34.

7. THE WAR OF 1847

1. Quoted in Irving W. Levinson, *Wars within War: Mexican Guerrillas, Domestic Elites, and the United States of America, 1846–1848* (Fort Worth, Tex.: Texas Christian University Press, 2005), 104.

2. José Fernando Ramírez, *Mexico During the War with the United States*, ed. Walter V. Scholes, tr. Elliott B. Scherr (Columbia: University of Missouri, 1950), 121.

3. Letter of August 26, 1846, in ibid., 55.

4. Ramirez, *Mexico During the War*, 77.

5. Quoted in Wilfrid Hardy Callcott, *Church and State in Mexico, 1822–1857* (New York: Octagon Books, 1971), 141.

6. Ramírez, *Mexico During the War*, 135.

7. Santiago Méndez to James Buchanan, March 25, 1848, in William R. Manning, *Diplomatic Correspondence of the United States: Inter-American Affairs*, vol. 8, *1831–1860* (Washington, D.C.: Carnegie Endowment for International Peace, 1937), 1071–72.

8. Nicholas Trist to James Buchanan, October 25 and December 26, 1847, in ibid., 958–59 and 1025–27.

9. Quoted in Thomas R. Hietala, *Manifest Design: American Exceptionalism and Empire*, rev. ed. (Ithaca, N.Y.: Cornell University Press, 1985), 162.

10. Quoted in David M. Pletcher, *The Diplomacy of Annexation: Texas, Oregon, and the Mexican War* (Columbia, Mo.: University of Missouri Press, 1973), 551.

11. Hietala, *Manifest Design*, 165.

EPILOGUE AND CONCLUSION

1. Quoted in Chaplain W. Morrison, *Democratic Politics and Sectionalism: The Wilmot Proviso Controversy* (Chapel Hill: University of North Carolina Press, 1967), 65.
2. Justo Sierra, *The Political Evolution of the Mexican People*, tr. Charles Ramsdell (Austin: University of Texas Press, 1969), 247.
3. John Lynch, *Caudillos in Spanish America, 1800–1850* (Oxford: Clarendon Press, 1992), 357.
4. Quoted in Gene Brack, *Mexico Views Manifest Destiny, 1821–1846: An Essay on the Origins of the Mexican War* (Albuquerque: University of New Mexico Press, 1975), 164.
5. José Fernando Ramírez, *Mexico During the War with the United States*, ed. Walter V. Scholes, tr. Elliott B. Scherr (Columbia: University of Missouri Studies, 1950), 122.
6. Quoted in Brack, *Mexico Views*, 154.
7. Terán quoted in Alleine Howren, "Causes and Origin of the Decree of April 6, 1830," *Southwestern Historical Quarterly* 16, no. 4 (April 1913), 400.
8. *El Siglo Diez y Nueve*, November 30, 1845.

SUGGESTIONS FOR
FURTHER READING

Comparisons between the United States and the nations of Latin America are surprisingly hard to come by. Some works that are quite useful in assessing the differences are Richard M. Morse, *New World Soundings: Culture and Ideology in the Americas* (Baltimore: Johns Hopkins University Press, 1989); David A. Brading, *The First America: The Spanish Monarchy, Creole Patriots and the Liberal State, 1492–1867* (Cambridge: Cambridge University Press, 1991); Lester D. Langley, *America in the Americas: The United States in the Western Hemisphere* (Athens: University of Georgia Press, 1989) and *The Americas in the Age of Revolution, 1750–1850* (New Haven, Conn.: Yale University Press, 1996).

On Mexico's path to independence, see Hugh M. Hamill, Jr., *The Hidalgo Revolt: Prelude to Mexican Independence* (Gainesville: University of Florida Press, 1966); Nettie Lee Benson, *The Provincial Deputation in Mexico: Harbinger of Provincial Autonomy, Independence, and Federalism* (Austin: University of Texas Press, 1992); Jaime Rodriguez O., ed., *The Independence of Mexico and the Creation of the New Nation* (Los Angeles: UCLA Latin American Center Publications; Irvine: Mexico/Chicano Program, University of California, 1989); Timothy Anna, *The Fall of the Royal Government in Mexico City* (Lincoln: University of Nebraska Press, 1978) and *The Mexican Empire of Iturbide* (Lincoln: University of Nebraska Press, 1990); William Spence Robinson, *Iturbide of Mexico* (Durham, N.C.: Duke University Press, 1952). For those seeking an in-depth social history of Mexican independence, focusing especially on the struggle's early years, see Eric Van Young, *The Other Rebellion: Popular Violence, Ide-*

ology, and the Mexican Struggle for Independence, 1810–1821 (Stanford, Calif.: Stanford University Press, 2001).

The literature on Manifest Destiny is vast. Some of the classics include Frederick Merk, *Manifest Destiny and Mission in American History: A Reinterpretation* (New York: Vintage Books, 1963); Albert K. Weinberg, *Manifest Destiny: A Study of Nationalist Expansion in American History* (Baltimore: Johns Hopkins University Press, 1935). For a good introduction to the topic, see Anders Stephanson, *Manifest Destiny: American Expansionism and the Empire of Right* (New York: Hill & Wang, 1995). A provocative reinterpretation of the topic is Thomas R. Hietala, *Manifest Design: American Exceptionalism and Empire*, rev. ed. (Ithaca, N.Y.: Cornell University Press, 1985). A very sophisticated account of Manifest Destiny as experienced by the people of Texas and New Mexico is Andrés Reséndez, *Changing National Identities at the Frontier: Texas and New Mexico, 1800–1850* (Cambridge: Cambridge University Press, 2005).

On the early years of U.S.-Mexican relations, see William R. Manning, *Early Diplomatic Relations Between the United States and Mexico* (Baltimore: Johns Hopkins University Press, 1913). For a brief overview, see Virginia Guedea and Jaime E. Rodríguez O., "How Relations between Mexico and the United States Began," in Rodríguez O. and Kathryn Vincent, eds., *Myths, Misdeeds, and Misunderstandings: The Roots of Conflict in U.S.-Mexican Relations* (Wilmington, Del.: Scholarly Resources, 1997), 17–46. On Joel Poinsett, see J. Fred Rippy, *Joel R. Poinsett, Versatile American* (Durham, N.C.: Duke University Press, 1935). For Poinsett's own early impressions of Mexico, see *Notes on Mexico, Made in the Autumn of 1822. Accompanied by a Historical Sketch of the Revolution* (Philadelphia: H.S. Carey and I. Lea, 1824). For the case against Poinsett, see José Fuentes Mares, *Poinsett: Historia de una gran intriga*, 4th ed. (Mexico: Editorial Jus, 1964).

On Texas, some useful works are Nettie Lee Benson, "Texas as Viewed from Mexico, 1820–1834," *Southwestern Historical Quarterly* 90, no. 3 (January 1987), 219–91, and her "Territorial Integrity in Mexican Politics, 1821–1833," in Jaime Rodríguez O., ed., *The Independence of Mexico and the Creation of the New Nation* (Los Angeles: UCLA Latin American Center, 1989), 275–307; Josefina Zoraida Vázquez, "The Colonization and Loss of Texas: A Mexican Perspective," in Rodríguez O. and Vincent, *Myths, Misdeeds, and Misunder-*

standings; Andreas V. Reichstein, *Rise of the Lone Star: The Making of Texas*, tr. Jeanne R. Wilson (College Station: Texas A&M University Press, 1989). A broad view can be found in David J. Weber's *The Mexican Frontier, 1821–1846: The American Southwest Under Mexico* (Albuquerque: University of New Mexico Press, 1982). For Texas (and related Mexican) history, an indispensable online source is the Texas Historical Association's *Handbook of Texas On-line*, which can be found at www.tsha.utexas.edu/handbook/online/.

On General Terán and the Texas Boundary Commission, see Jack Jackson, ed., *Texas by Terán: The diary kept by General Manuel de Mier y Terán on his 1828 Inspection of Texas*, tr. John Wheat (Austin: University of Texas Press, 2000); Ohland Morton, *Terán and Texas: A Chapter in Texas-Mexican Relations* (Austin: Texas State Historical Association, 1948); José María Sánchez, "A Trip to Texas in 1828," tr. Carlos E. Casteneda, *Southwestern Historical Quarterly* 29, no. 4 (April 1926), 249–88; and Jean Louis Berlandier, *Journey to Mexico During the Years 1826 to 1834*, tr. Sheila M. Ohlendorf, Josette M. Bigelow, Mary M. Standifer (Austin: Texas State Historical Association, 1980).

On Stephen F. Austin, the classic treatment is Eugene C. Barker, *The Life of Stephen F. Austin, Founder of Texas, 1793–1836: A Chapter in the Westward Movement of the Anglo-American People* (Austin: University of Texas Press, 1926). For a more recent assessment, see Gregg Cantrell, *Stephen F. Austin, Empresario of Texas* (New Haven, Conn.: Yale University Press, 1999). On the Republic of Texas, see Stanley Siegel, *A Political History of the Texas Republic, 1836–1845* (Austin: University of Texas Press, 1956); Joseph Milton Nance, *After San Jacinto: The Texas-Mexican Frontier, 1836–1841* (Austin: University of Texas Press, 1963); and *Attack and Counterattack: The Texas-Mexican Frontier, 1842* (Austin: University of Texas Press, 1964).

On the political history of Mexico during the years from independence to the U.S.-Mexican War, see Jesús Reyes Heroles, *El liberalismo mexicano*, 3 vols. (Mexico: Fondo de Cultura Económica, 1974); Stanley C. Green, *The Mexican Republic: The First Decade, 1823–1832* (Pittsburgh: University of Pittsburgh Press, 1987); Donald Fithian Stevens, *Origins of Instability in Early Republican Mexico* (Durham, N.C.: Duke University Press, 1991); Michael Costeloe, *Primera república federal de México, 1824–1835: un estudio de los par-*

tidos políticos en el México independiente, tr. Manuel Fernández Gasalla (Mexico: Fondo de Cultura Económica, 1975); Timothy Anna, *Forging Mexico, 1821–1835* (Lincoln: University of Nebraska Press, 1998); Harold Dana Sims, *The Expulsion of Mexico's Spaniards, 1821–1836* (Pittsburgh: University of Pittsburgh Press, 1990); Josefina Zoraida Vázquez, ed., *El establecimiento del federalismo en México, 1821–1827* (Mexico: Colegio de México, 2003); Michael Costeloe, *The Central Republic in Mexico, 1835–1846: Hombres de Bien in the Age of Santa Anna* (Cambridge: Cambridge University Press, 1993); Barbara Tenenbaum, *The Politics of Penury: Debts and Taxes in Mexico, 1821–1856* (Albuquerque: University of New Mexico Press, 1986). Some biographies of key figures are Wilfrid Hardy Callcott, *Santa Anna: The Story of an Enigma Who Once Was Mexico* (Hamden, Conn.: Archon Books, 1964); Okah Jones, *Santa Anna* (New York: Twayne Publishers, 1968); John Lynch, *Caudillos in Spanish America, 1800–1850* (Oxford: Clarendon Press, 1992); C. Alan Hutchinson, "Valentín Gómez Farías: A Biographic Study," Ph.D. diss., University of Texas at Austin, 1948; Thomas E. Cotner, *The Military and Political Career of José Joaquín de Herrera, 1792–1854* (New York: Greenwood Press, 1969). A classic intellectual history of the period is Charles Hale, *Mexican Liberalism in the Age of Mora, 1821–1853* (New Haven, Conn.: Yale University Press, 1968).

On the diplomacy surrounding the annexation of Texas and the start of the war, see George Rives, *The United States and Mexico, 1821–1848*, 2 vols. (New York: Charles Scribner's Sons, 1913); Justin Harvey Smith, *The Annexation of Texas* (New York: Barnes & Noble, 1941); and especially David M. Pletcher, *The Diplomacy of Annexation: Texas, Oregon, and the Mexican War* (Columbia, Mo.: University of Missouri Press, 1973).

On politics in Mexico surrounding the war, two recent books are extremely helpful: Pedro Santoni, *Mexicans at Arms: Puro Federalists and the Politics of War, 1845–1848* (Fort Worth: Texas Christian University Press, 1996); and Irving Levinson, *Wars Within War: Mexican Guerrillas, Domestic Elites, and the United States of America, 1846–1848* (Fort Worth: Texas Christian University Press, 2005). Also see Luis Fernando Granados, *Sueñan las piedras: Alzamiento ocurrido en la ciudad de México, 14, 15 y 16 de septiembre de 1847* (Mexico: Ediciones Era, 2003). A useful personal account of life in Mexico City during the war is José Fernando Ramírez, *Mexico During the War with the United States*, ed. Walter V. Scholes, tr. Elliott B. Scherr (Columbia: University of Missouri, 1950). Classic accounts of 1840s Mexico by foreign observers are Fanny Calderón de la Barca, *Life in Mexico* (Berkeley: University of California Press, 1982); and Brantz Mayer, *Mexico as It Was and as It Is* (New York: J. Winchester, 1844).

General histories of the war have tended to concentrate on military matters and the United States point of view. See Justin Harvey Smith, *The War With Mexico*, 2 vols. (New York: Macmillan, 1919); Jack Bauer, *The Mexican War, 1846–1848* (New York: Macmillan, 1974); Otis A. Singletary, *The Mexican War* (Chicago: University of Chicago Press, 1960); John S. D. Eisenhower, *So Far From God: The U.S. War with Mexico, 1846–1848* (New York: Doubleday, 1989). A good encyclopedia of the war is Donald S. Frazier, ed., *The United States and Mexico at War: Nineteenth Century Expansion and Conflict* (New York: Macmillan Reference Books, 1998).

For an excellent interpretive essay on the war from the Mexican viewpoint, see Gene Brack, *Mexico Views Manifest Destiny, 1821–1846: An Essay on the Origins of the Mexican War* (Albuquerque: University of New Mexico Press, 1975). A good collection of translated Mexican writings about the war is Cecil Robinson, ed. and trans., *The View from Chapultepec: Mexican Writers on the Mexican American War* (Tucson: University of Arizona Press, 1989). A contemporaneous account of the Mexican side of the war is Ramón Alcaraz, *The Other Side: Notes for the History of the War Between Mexico and the United States*, tr. and ed. by Albert C. Ramsey (New York: John Riley, 1850). Mexican memoirs of the war include Carlos María de Bustamante, *El Nuevo Bernal Díaz del Castillo, o sea Historia de la invasión de los anglo-americanos en México* (Imprenta de V. García Torres, 1847); and Guillermo Prieto, *Memoria de mis tiempos . . .* , 2 vols. (Mexico and Paris: Vda. de C. Bouret, 1906).

On the impact of the war in the United States, see Joel H. Silbey, *Storm over Texas: The Annexation Controversy and the Road to Civil War* (Oxford: Oxford University Press, 2005); for a brief and very readable account, see Michael F. Holt, *The Fate of Their Country: Politicians, Slavery Extension, and the Coming of the Civil War* (New York: Hill & Wang, 2004). For the impact on Mexico, see Charles H. Hale, "The War with the United States and the Crisis in Mexican Thought," *Americas* 14, no. 2 (October 1957). On the Treaty of Guadalupe Hidalgo and its impact, see Richard Griswold del

Castillo, *The Treaty of Guadalupe Hidalgo: A Legacy of Conflict* (Norman: University of Oklahoma Press, 1990).

WEBSITES

www.dmwv.org/mexwar/mexwar1.htm (website of the Descendants of Mexican War veterans)

www.aztecclub.com/ (website of the Aztec Club of 1847; some good information and artwork)

www.pbs.org/kera/usmexicanwar/war/ (excellent PBS site on the war)

www.tsha.utexas.edu/handbook/online/index.html (Handbook of Texas Online)

www.latinamericanstudies.org/mexican.htm (excellent website on Latino Studies compiled by Dr. Antonio Rafael de la Cova; many primary documents, maps, timelines, etc.)

ACKNOWLEDGMENTS

For various suggestions and bits of help along the way, I am grateful to Gil Joseph, Doug Murphy, Peter Bower, Bill Schell, Scott Nelson, Ben Fallaw, and Rafael de la Cova. I also wish to thank the librarians at Auburn University Montgomery who helped me obtain many hard-to-find books that were essential to my research, especially Jeanette Lessels and Carolyn Johnson; and the folks at AUM's Technology Resource Center for help with scanning. Thanks are also due to June Kim of Hill and Wang for her patience and insightful advice. My greatest debts are to my wife, Karren Pell, who read the entire manuscript and offered invaluable suggestions, and to John Chasteen, who got me started on the project in the first place.

INDEX